CIRCLE 'ROUND THE SQUARE

Pictures from an Iowa childhood

By Dorothy Daniel

Traveling salesmen who came through Iowa used to call Indianola "The Holy City," and they tried their level best to finish up their business in time to catch the night train back to Des Moines. It was true — at least around 1912 — that there was no saloon, no dance hall, no pool hall, and no place to bowl or buy cigarettes. And the film emporium was looked upon locally as a cesspool of the devil. But the natives of Indianola had plenty of compensations.

For example, if you were an indigent member of a minority group like the Democratic party, you could get your teeth fixed free, because Doc Mullican was a crusading Democrat. You could hear the lecturers who

(continued on back flap)

Wilfred Funk, Inc., 153 E. 24th St., N. Y. 10

CIRCLE 'ROUND THE SQUARE

drawings by Sam Kweskin

CIRCLE 'ROUND THE SQUARE

Pictures from an Iowa Childhood

BY DOROTHY DANIEL

WILFRED FUNK, INC., NEW YORK

For Bun of course

CONTENTS

1   The Noon Whistle   3

2   The Square   38

3   From Schimmelpfennig's to the Empress   58

4   Mr. Brown and Mr. White   80

5   John Wesley and the Seventh Day   100

6   The Arts and the Mullicans   138

7   Social Security   158

8   My Dear Professor   193

9   The Secret   218

CIRCLE 'ROUND THE SQUARE

I

THE NOON WHISTLE

On Monday, June 29, Grandfather brought the Des
Moines *Register* home at noon rolled up under his arm,
just as he did every day, Monday through Saturday,
every week in every year.

There was not a single notable thing about this day, except perhaps that it was unusually balmy. The Middle West can generate fiendish Julys, horrendous Augusts, insufferable Septembers, it is true. But June as a rule is warm and bright and clear, and sweet-scented, and the June of 1914 was no exception.

The hollyhocks were in bloom along the alley fence behind the wood shed, hiding the spot where Grandfather dug the big hole to bury the garbage.

Squirrels were jumping from bough to branch carrying on their incessant chattering warfare with their loud-mouthed companions, the blue jays.

We were engaged in a project out beyond the lattice fence called "Artist." There was a pile of broken and weathered shingles and some new slabs left over from when the house had been rebuilt. We were painting these with a sloppy kind of liquid concocted principally of mud and water. Our masterpieces were lined along the hedge of white phlox and ribbon grass that separated our yard from Clarence Reynolds' moss rose bushes.

The noon whistle shrieked and we shivered.

We always shivered when the noon whistle shrieked.

The noon whistle let go with a blast that penetrated the sun-spattered darkness of the furthermost privy out Des Moines Road and clattered the teacups on the pantry shelves as far off as the fairgrounds.

A steam whistle it was, a mysterious by-product of the "light house," where great green wheels whirred around in shining covers to produce a thin, wavering trickle of a modern miracle, electricity.

The whistle had other tones and other uses, all of them dominating and spine-tingling. When there was a fire the siren screamed up and down the scale from a low, shuddering bass to a high, shrill, ear-splitting treble. Scootie, Grandfather's ancient, graying Irish terrier, sat out on the front steps and howled. Bun, who had only been born in 1912, ran to bury her tow-head under the crocheted afghan on Grandmother's couch.

Then there would be a breathless silence as the siren paused and we waited for the staccato toots that told us where the fire was.

One . . . two . . . three. . . . Third Ward—out by the college!

Grandmother would never let us go to the fires for fear we'd get hurt, but soon after the identifying toots there would be a patter of feet on the sidewalk and we would go to stand on the porch and yell out, "Where is it?"

And Don Berry or Kenneth Brown or Jay Berg-stresser would go by, calling over his shoulder, "Mc-Coy's Barn!" or "Halliday's hayloft!" and off he and the rest would go to see what they could do in the emergency.

Fires were the worst, but the call for the sheriff was almost as bad. The siren started the run of the scale and then stopped short with four short toots. Its authority was such that only a raid by masked bandits or a bloody murder would seem a good enough reason to call the sheriff so urgently, but sober reflection brought us to the resigned and disappointed realization that Indianola wasn't a logical place for such violence.

No one of any real interest had been locked up in our jail since the notorious murders of Tear-Down Hill, when Grandfather's Uncle Robert Parrott had been the counsel for the defense.

Assorted vagrants were sometimes discovered in the straw of cattle cars, but no real "criminal" had ever known our jail. Even the "Tear-Down" murders had resulted from a feud, which was, according to Grandfather, more a difference of opinion carried to extravagant lengths than any real felony.

"Who do you think it is?" we would ask Grandfather when the sheriff's whistle let go, and he would laugh and say, "Nobody. Hartzler's wife's just hunting him for dinner. That's the hot-biscuit toot." But it always sounded like a bank-holdup blast to us.

The whistle also blew for six o'clock and curfew, and on those charmed and crystal mornings when it was either too cold or the snow drifts were too high to open school for the day. Six o'clock was announced with a rumbling bass blast similar to noon. "No school" was four shorts about eight in the morning. Curfew had a tremolo calculated to send children scurrying home in a proper frame of mind for their bedside prayers.

On Monday, June 29, the noon whistle let go as

usual. We put down our muddy paint brushes and
separated for dinner.

Screen doors banged rhythmically all along the
street as children went in the back doors, at the com-
mand of the whistle, to wash their hands and faces at
the sinks and get ready for their dinners; and as fa-
thers and grandfathers stepped up on the front porches
and banged the screen doors behind them.

Grandfather's routine was always the same. He
would appear, meat under one arm and the Des Moines
Register under the other, go out to the kitchen, say
"Good morning, Madam" to Grandmother, take the
water bucket off the stool, and go outside to the well
stoop. If there was any water left in the bucket he
would throw it out over Grandmother's bed of golden-
glow. Then he would prime, coax, and conjure the old
pump until ice-cold, clear water gushed into the white
porcelain bucket. Then he would carry the bucket into
the house, put it on the stool, hang his hat on a hook
behind the door, and go into the library to read until
Grandmother fried the meat.

We had cherished our well with the old oaken bucket
for a long time, but the neighbors' cats were forever
falling in, and Grandmother, who was a great one
for cats, was also a stickler for sanitation. So she got
Clarence Reynolds to cap the well and we had a pump.
It didn't work very well—in fact it didn't work at all
unless you attacked it with the enthusiasm of a young
lover and the physical violence of a Japanese wrestler
—but we did have a pump.

I would put the water in the glasses and take the covers off the butter, preserves, apple sauce, and pickles, and Bun would put the napkins around. She was good at that. She would help herself to a toothpick from Grandfather's toothpick holder and Grandmother would say, "Tell him." And Bun would run as fast as she could and stand in the doorway of the library. After a while he would look up and see her and say, "Well, Bunny, did Grandmother send for me?" And Bun would beam and nod. And that's pretty much the way it was every day.

Even on the twenty-ninth of June, 1914, that's the way it was. We had fried round steak and mashed potatoes and gravy and asparagus and macaroni and cheese, and hot biscuits and pickled beets, and Grandfather talked about some fool thing "Wilson" had done, and said something about an Austrian named Ferdinand getting shot. He also said Doc Mullican was getting too big for his britches. Then he asked me if I was ready to collect the dollar he was paying me to read *Kenilworth*.

After dinner he went back uptown to his office, and we got the dishes done and Grandmother went to take her nap and we went back to our mud painting.

We quickly forgot Grandfather's brief mention of "Ferdinand." During that month of July we naturally heard the word "war" used rather frequently, but it was a word that belonged in adult conversations or in history books, so we paid no attention to it. At least, we paid no attention until August 1, 1914—and that

wasn't because of the war exactly but because of Dr.
Mullican.

When the noon whistle blew on that first day of August we were playing "hollyhock ladies," having long since run completely out of shingles. We were sitting on the grass in the shade of the old black-walnut tree.

Hollyhock ladies, in season, are more fun than paper dolls because they permit an ingenuity of design lacking in the static, slick females to be cut out of Sears, Roebuck catalogs or *Delineator* magazines. The basic requirements for hollyhock ladies are hollyhock blossoms and a paper of pins. The bud end of the flower is the neck, from which a bouffant skirt of pink or white or deep red falls away to floor length. A round, fat seed pod becomes the head, with the smaller flower buds serving as arms. Sometimes we used ribbon grass for sashes and the seeding end of blue grass for plumes. White clover we braided into stoles, and yellow sorrel was just the right size for hat trimming and shoulder corsages.

These elegant ladies were titled, arrogant, and indolent, and they spent their days at tea parties and charity balls and did not seem to mind when their dresses faded with the night, for their costumes were renewable, each dawn bringing the bounty of a completely new wardrobe.

The dressmaking shop for hollyhock ladies always shut down abruptly when the raucous noonday whistle burst through the warm golden quiet of Indianola, Iowa, catapulting old Mr. Flummer out of his rocker

and rattling the crocks in the potting shed at the cemetery.

On this first day of August, 1914, at noon, we
quickly lined up our hollyhock ladies in a neat row for
what we hoped was a quadrille, and disbanded for
dinner.

Zora Stewart was spending the summer with her
grandmother, Mona Clayton, who lived two houses
over. Her grandfather had fought in the Civil War. He
was a beautiful old man with snow-white hair who sat
in a wicker rocker in the sun of the side porch and told
us all about the horrors of Gettysburg. Our Grandfather said "Clayton" had never been anywhere near
Gettysburg, but we put this down to jealousy because
Grandfather had been just too young to fight for the
Union. Grandfather called the old gentleman "Benny,"
which was a liberty no one else dared to take with the
Colonel. Despite certain fairly violent differences of
opinion concerning the Army of the Potomac and the
Western Campaign, both men were regularly-attend-
ing members of the Bible Club, and they lived together
quite comfortably as neighbors so long as Clarence
Reynolds lived between them.

Catherine Carpenter lived next door across the alley. She had a black and white pony named Ione who
despised people and could rarely be ridden to saddle
because she was almost constantly in-a-family-way.

All three of us—Zora, Catherine, and I—had little
sisters. Becky Stewart and Betty Carpenter were dark-

haired and gay. My sister was tow-headed and solemn. Grandmother had started right off calling her "my precious little bunny-rabbit," so Bunny she was and Bun she became.

Grandmother thought it was a "fright" the way we duped the little sisters into running our errands for us. We sent them as far down the alley as Sigler's and Berry's for bachelor's-buttons and verbena, and over the fence to Proudfoot's arbor for grape leaves.

This particular morning Grandmother had baked a special batch of cookies: thin little sugar cookies cut out in the shapes of robins with clove eyes and lions with cinnamon-and-sugar manes, fat little women with allspice eyes, and straddle-legged men with shirt buttons made of bright red candy.

"Let the little honey B's take first," she said, offering us the big pan of oven-hot cookies. Grandmother was a great one for puns, the underdog, and serving food at a temperature sufficient to give the unwary third-degree burns. She held the hot pan firmly with a pot holder neatly quilted from the scraps left over from Aunt Dot's latest cotton housedress. Aunt Dot had never in her life worn a housedress, and ever since she married George Smith and went to live in Idaho she wore overalls, but Grandmother thought she should wear a housedress and kept sending them to her. Grandfather said maybe George wore them, but that seemed unlikely.

The cookies had long since disappeared down "red

lane" and Grandmother was back in the kitchen frying thin crispy strips of white cornmeal mush when the whistle blew for noon.

Screen doors began to bang, including ours.

"Where is Grandfather?" I said. "The whistle blew."

"I don't know," she said. "He was to bring the meat."

Usually Grandfather stopped at Schimmelpfennig's on the way home and brought the round steak wrapped up in a stout brown paper package. This would be his second trip home that day. He rose early, at four or five o'clock, and without waking Grandmother he walked uptown to the office where, he said, he could get some work done before his clients started "bothering" him. Then, home for breakfast, he would tell us which stars were out and where the constellations were that morning before daybreak. Stars at night are as romantic as all getout, but with oatmeal at breakfast they are just stars.

Besides oatmeal and stars we had buckwheat cakes with sausage and sausage gravy, fried eggs, bacon, country syrup, hot biscuits, applesauce, marmalade, preserves, and hot cocoa, coffee, tea, or milk.

Buckwheat cakes are properly started in the fall and left to keep pace with the season. About the time red haws become edible, which is after a first frost but before a killer, Grandmother would put down the buckwheat. There is nothing very mysterious about this first rite. She would take a yeast cake and break it up in a

cup half full of lukewarm water, add a half-teaspoonful
of sugar, and stir until it was all dissolved. This solu-
tion was dumped into a good-sized yellow crockery
bowl that held two cups of buckwheat flour, a table-
spoonful of salt, and two tablespoonfuls of molasses,
and all was stirred together vigorously with two cups
of buttermilk. The bowl was covered with a clean cloth
and placed squarely on top of the hot-air register in
the dining room. The following morning she would give
the batter a few hearty stirs with a wooden spoon, then
drop blobs as big as a plate onto the hot griddle that
had been greased just a bit with a piece of bacon rind.
The thin, round cakes were served hot, crisp, and lacy
with new sorghum made right there in Warren County.

The trick was to have more buckwheat batter than
there was call for cakes. Grandmother took what was
left in the bowl, added more salt, a touch of sorghum, a
couple of handfuls of buckwheat, diluted the mass with
buttermilk or sour milk, and put it back to rise again.
By Thanksgiving the buckwheat was getting fairly
tart and sounding pretty snappy as Grandmother beat
it down in the mornings. And by the middle of January,
when cold weather set in, it was hard to tell whether it
was the pancakes or the sorghum that was making the
china ducks above the plate-rail flap their wings that
way.

Buckwheat got retired on Easter Saturday, giving
way to cornmeal—on account, she said, of the weevils.
This was just her way of saying she was tired of
thrashing the buckwheat batter down to consistency

every morning, for not even the healthiest weevil could have lived long in Grandmother's spring buckwheat batter. And no child could manage his way to school over the old brick sidewalk without colliding with at least one maple tree after a platter of March buckwheats.

They never fazed Grandfather, though. He could stash away a stack of eight as usual even when they got so strong you could have set a match to them and called them crepes-suzettes. Ballasted by buckwheats, he walked uptown to the barber shop, where Frank Chapman shaved him with a straight-edge razor and commented on the latest runaway. Frank and Grandfather shared a secret. They were both violently afraid of horses. But their long friendship almost came to an unhappy end the day Frank succumbed to Mrs. Chapman's demand for an automobile. Grandfather thought Frank was getting soft, and took comfort in the fact that his friend smashed two fenders and blew a tire his first time out.

When Frank had finished with him, Grandfather would go around the corner to the wide, open stairs that led to the second floor of the Indianola Bank Building, and, tucking Scoot up under his arm, he would mount the stairs with the brisk and determined air of a man who enjoys his work and knows he is good at it.

Three rooms comprised Grandfather's offices. The front room, the one with the door that read "O. C. Brown, Attorney-at-Law," was on the corner and had windows on two sides that looked out across the square toward the courthouse. In the corner of this room was the high pigeon-hole desk which housed mysteries of deeds and mortgages and notes and curiously folded legal papers with strange-sounding names. There was a paperweight that had a picture of Lincoln under glass and also, in a tinglingly special drawer, a piece of tanned human skin about six inches long that Grandmother wouldn't have in the house.

His desk chair was a high-backed black leather beast that pitched and rolled and bucked on its swivel, but the low-backed spindle chairs that faced the courthouse lawn in a neat row opposite the corner windows were comfortable and sturdy.

The middle room was for clients. And whether to impress them or to conserve space, or maybe both, books lined this room from floor to ceiling, with only slight concession for windows and doors. There was a long oak table in the center of all these elegantly bound books, and enough high-backed oak chairs to hold a board meeting.

The third room was for a clerk when there was one, supplies, ink, envelopes, a letter-press, files, and—because Sam White was a particularly neat custodian—the third room contained an orderly arrangement of uniquely disassociated objects, to wit: a stuffed bald eagle, a large framed lithograph of "Milton Dictating to his Daughters," a bough of a tree complete with stuffed squirrel and nest, a model of Professor Sedgwick's chronograph, ditto his train-stopper, a clock with chuckle-headed men in it representing Grandfather and friends, a Chinese umbrella stand with dragons, a picture of Uncle Robert Parrott, a yellow guitar, a pair of Indian clubs with gold and black ribbons, and things like that. They were mostly treasures that clients had given him and Grandmother wouldn't let him bring home.

There was a big octagonal clock that hung on the wall in the front office opposite the desk. It had a pendulum and the soft, unfaltering tick of doom. Even its strike was as nervously prying as a cruise director: "What did you get done this last hour? Or are you the same lazy good-for-nothing you were at half-past?"

All this officious timekeeping bothered Grandfather not a bit. He was just a couple of pebbles away from being stone deaf.

But he could see well enough, and when the long hand got to eleven-thirty, Grandfather stood up, no matter who was in the office, put on his hat, peered across the tops of the maple trees to check the time on the courthouse clock, and started for the post office and Schimmelpfennig's butcher shop.

Many a client found himself midway through ". . . and I says to him," only to look around and find Grandfather gone, the door closed, and the pendulum wagging away on the wall with a condescending rebuke in every tock.

We never quite understood how Grandfather had any clients at all. He was brusque and bitingly sarcastic. He would not permit smoking in his office. He would take only those cases in which he felt a client had been wronged in the face of the law. His sense of protecting the widow and the orphan bordered on the neurotic, but even the most aggrieved client could be made to feel like a culprit under Grandfather's searching, steel-blue-eyed inquisition. When Grandmother said, "I don't see why they come to you at all!" he would reply with a twinkle in his eye, and on one memorable occasion a pinch on Grandmother's bottom, "Because I'm the best gosh-dinged lawyer in the state of Iowa, and I've forgotten more law than Frank Henderson will ever know." This was not strictly accurate, since Grandfather never forgot anything he knew. However, it was a fact that people said he would have been a judge long ago if he hadn't been so hard of hearing.

Contrary to the idea that anyone over thirty seems very old indeed to the very young, neither Grandfather nor Grandmother seemed even "elderly" to me. He was tall and neither thin nor fat. He walked like a man who had enjoyed years of military service, which he had not. His head was round as a billiard ball—"punkin-head Irish" he called it—and his hair was white, soft, and wavy. He had a gray, closely clipped mustache and skin that looked pink clean even when it was grimy dirty. Everybody in Indianola was just a little afraid of him except Grandmother and me and Scoot and Doc Mullican.

Scoot was a black but graying Irish terrier with tobacco juice dribbling out the corner of his mouth and the breath of an open sewer. He had belonged to Uncle

Bobby, and it was during those early puppy days that somebody had shot him in the hip. Thereafter he went on three legs. Grandfather called him a mathematician dog because he put down three and carried one. Scoot went everywhere Grandfather did: up West Ashland, around the square to the post office, into the courthouse and the courtroom, and home again.

Scoot was the only dog permitted to sit in the courts of law and equity. When he had been a young dog, visiting judges had ordered him out. The bailiff was afraid of Scoot, having had one unfortunate encounter from which he still bore scars in a place where they by custom had to remain hidden. Grandfather pretended he was too hard of hearing to understand the order, and the judges gave up. English law being built on precedent, it soon became legal for Scoot to appear in court. After a bit it became law itself; once Judge Applegate held up court for ten minutes until Scoot got there, because he said there was no use starting until Scoot got comfortable. His entrance always distracted the jurors.

After he got to be sixteen or seventeen years old he developed a kind of heart murmur, so Grandfather carried him up the wide, steep stairs to the office and to the courtroom.

Before Scoot died he had a lifetime season pass to the Empress and never missed a show. When Dorothy Mullican got to pounding out the battle or escape or chase 'em music, Scoot would sometimes lift his head and give a few sharp barks and a bay or two, but this only heightened the effect of pursuit.

Scoot's privileges were much like those extended to dogs who in a later day were to lead the blind. In any event, the man and the dog were inseparable companions. They were accepted as a team, which they were. They simply liked being together, and Scoot would have been indignant at the thought that, because he told Grandfather when the phone rang or when people were coming up the steps or when a galloping team was heading for them or when Grandmother called them to dinner, he was anything so practical as a hearing-ear dog. He was proud of his contribution to the partnership and he was embarrassed when he had to be carried, but he understood this, too, and suffered the indignity with good grace.

Grandfather wore carefully tailored suits of the cut known later as "ivy league," one white shirt a week, the cuffs of which he was proud to turn, a black string tie, and a heavy gold watch and chain.

The fact that he was almost stone deaf did not in the least dampen his enthusiasm for music. He liked music of any kind, tempo, voice, instrument, arrangement, or rendition. He went on the theory that there is no bad music—some is just better than others and any music is better than no music at all. We grew up to argue this premise with him but we couldn't win. When you feel that way about a person or a thing it goes deeper than reason.

There was a kind of high window ledge in his library that faced out toward Reynolds', and these windows were leaded with stained glass panes simulating, certainly not depicting, tiger lilies.

It was along this ledge, which was book-deep, that he kept his mouth organs. He had mouth organs of every key, shape, size, and manufacture. There were great double-decked affairs about twelve inches long that he could make sound like church organs. And there was one Aunt Margaret had given him with golden horns along the edge. Some were gold and some were silver, some were narrow and some were fat, but the ones he liked best were the little fellows he could hold close in his hands and make sound like a trumpet in the cup of his palm. When life was treating him right he would take off his coat, pull up his sleeves, and cut loose on a mouth harp, walking back and forth through the house from kitchen to front hall executing intricate tap steps to the tune of "Tara's Halls," "Arkansas Traveler," "Irish Washerwoman," or "The Bonnie Blue Flag." We were quite grown and had moved to Chicago before we discovered that a mouth harp can be played from a sitting position.

But on this August day in 1914 there were no toe-tapping sounds from the hall, no trilling scales or flutey arpeggios to accompany the popping mush in Grandmother's skillet.

"Maybe a client kept him," Grandmother said. "It doesn't matter. We can have the steak for supper with eggs. He'll like that." She stooped to open the oven door. "We've got the beans and roasting ears I got off of Mr. Burkett's wagon and I've made macaroni and cheese. Cut some cold ham and put on some pickled beets and watermelon preserves. At least we can look like we are having a dinner after all." She poked her finger into the top of a hot baking-powder biscuit to see if it was done. It was, and she lifted the biscuits out and slid them onto the back of the stove. A thick apple pie bubbled over in the oven, its sugary juice dripping down to sizzle on the hot iron grill. She moved it over to the right, away from the fire box. "I guess we'll have enough without the meat," she said. "Papa doesn't have much of an appetite these hot days. We can make do."

Grandmother was not much taller than I, barely over five feet. She wore her dark-brown hair in an intricate arrangement of puffs and curls over the top of her head. This day, as always, she wore a stiffly starched housedress with short sleeves, and an apron with a bib that went around her neck. This particular apron was cross-stitched with red. The pattern was supposed to have come out looking like a plate and a cup with knife and fork. I had made it for her for Christmas. In a moment of enthusiasm I had added my own legend to the design. "I love you!" was what had been intended, but the effect was that of four young bantam roosters with foully bloody feet having wandered irresolutely across Grandmother's commodious lap.

She was chuffy, but of the build to be buxom. Still corseted in the style of the turn of the century, which meant that mysterious and disputed two years when things were not sure whether they belonged to one century or the other, Grandmother's bosom had the look of an ample shelf. Once long ago she had let me put my little iron stove on her chest, where it sat firmly and evenly, heaving only slightly as she breathed.

She had beautiful, small, capable hands and she was proud of her legs, her slender ankles, and her feet. She was as sleekly clean as a cat, but Grandfather, seeing her come walking down the street from Alonaidni, would smile when she came up on the porch and say, "How is Miss Jenny Wren this fine day?"

We all got to thinking of her as a wren, a small, round, brown wren, tripping along on diminutive feet. It was a good simile as similes go, but it did not go well with the fact that every picture we ever had of her had a cat in it. She had some cat or other all her life. She talked to them and they answered her. Neither lady nor cat made a fuss about it, but sometimes they affronted even those who loved them with their effortless cleanliness.

Grandfather was a great one for anecdote, his own or anybody else's: Julius Caesar's, Charles Lamb's, Washington Irving's, Abraham Lincoln's, it made no difference to him. An anecdote was an anecdote, and, like music, some were just more interesting than others. But Grandmother didn't talk much about her past or her childhood. Grandfather said it was because she hadn't had any, since he had married her when she was sixteen. We had a suspicion, though, that those first sixteen years had been exciting ones if we could just get her to tell us more about them. Sometimes we would say, "Grandmother, where did you get this old pewter pitcher?" And she would say, "Oh, I guess that came out in the wagon."

That it "came out in the wagon" meant that this particular piece of household equipment had originated in Maryland or Pennsylvania and had made the trip overland to Warren County in the Conestoga wagon with Grandmother, Uncle Willie, and Maggie Ellis. There the family settled down on a farm (part of a fifteen-hundred-acre tract that belonged to their grandfather Hallam) and waited for Indians.

Hamilton the irascible, Hamilton the dour, the father of this brood, gave farming back to the Indians in short order and took himself off over the countryside to build county courthouses and Methodist churches. His wife, Minerva, did not mind the Indians if she could be sure of seeing them first. Grandmother recalled her mother's saying it was enough to scare the gizzard out of you to look up from scrubbing the floor to see an old Indian watching you from the window. So she surrounded herself and her children with a covey of guinea hens as sentries, and always kept a supply of ginger cookies handy for when the Indians came to trade Oswego tea or sassafras root or a hatful of wild plums.

We thought maybe it was her mother's sorrow, which was cautiously referred to by our elders as "Minerva's Secret," that kept Grandmother from talking about the Indian days and the Conestoga wagon. Anyway, she almost never brought up the subject.

We had two kitchens, one for summer and one for winter.

In the summer Grandmother was supposed to use her kerosene stove in the summer kitchen, but she said the oven wasn't worth the powder and shot you'd need to blow it up with, so she always had Grandfather fire up the wood stove before he left for the office at four-thirty or five. After dinner, if the day was hot, she would let the fire die down and we would have a cold supper or something easily fried on the kerosene nuisance.

With the wood stove going the kitchen must have been a hundred and ten on that strange August first, but Grandmother looked as cool as though she had been sitting with us in the shade of the walnut tree. "Bring me the plates for the warming oven," she said. Proper service was proper service, hot or cold.

The old wood stove had a water reservoir at the side, a deep oven in the center, six stove eyes, and two warming ovens. You could as easily cook a dinner for twenty or thirty as for four once the fire was right, and nothing pleased Grandfather more than to have us all at home doing justice to "Jenny's cooking."

"I'll get the water," I said, after I had sliced the ham and put cut glass bowls filled with pickled beets and watermelon pickles on the table. I reached for the white porcelain bucket that stood in the corner on a high stool in the summer kitchen.

"No, let Grandfather do it," she said. "He likes to think he is helping, and besides the bucket is too heavy for you. Wash Bunny's face instead." She ladled a little hot rainwater out of the reservoir on the stove into the wash basin in the sink. We had a rainwater cistern and a pump on it. But first we filled the barrel. This was because the first rain washed off the roof, carrying leaves and box elder bugs and maple seed tails along with it, and if these got into the cistern they would clog up the pump or settle to the bottom and foul the water. So the rain spout had a two-way switch at the bottom. Turned one way the barrel filled up, then it was safe to switch the rainwater into the cistern. This moment usually came in the midst of a torrential inundation. Throwing an apron or a shawl or an old raincoat over her head, Aunt Margaret would make a dive for the rain spout. I took my turns at it, too, but usually they wouldn't let me because I got too wet.

The rainwater Grandmother put into the basin in the sink was from the cistern. You could tell that by its rich, brownish color and its musty smell of leaf mold. For no matter how quick Aunt Margaret was on the switch, leaves and locust blossoms and cottonwood boles, together with an occasional green walnut, were sure to get into the cistern.

I got a wash cloth from behind the door and went to find Bun.

She was sitting in the big bay of Grandmother's sitting room under the rim of a giant saw-tooth begonia that overflowed its brass jardiniere so that red and green fuzzy leaves on long stems cascaded nearly to the floor. Bun was slowly turning the leaves of a great book. "Zivil War!" she said, and she peered down at one of the elaborate etchings. "No Benny!" she added airily.

"Grandmother will Zivil-war you if you tear her book!" I said.

"Theze don't tear," she said confidently. Then, seeing the wash cloth, "I'm very bizzy."

The green window shades in the bay were drawn against the heat of noonday, and the stained glass transoms over the side door to the porch cast an eerie light on her blond head. There was a kind of tacit understanding that Grandmother's sitting room was Bun's sanctuary, as Grandfather's library was mine.

No matter where else we lived, this big square wooden ark of a house was always home to us. Here we spent our holidays and our summers and whatever other time seemed expedient in the random life of our parents. We stayed with Grandmother when Dad staked the claim in Idaho. We went to school in Indianola when Mother was selling fireless cookers in Nebraska, or defending the Indians in South Dakota, or writing for the Des Moines *Register* while our father and two Norwegians tried to introduce Swedish wall paper to the Germans in Minnesota.

If our being with Grandmother for long stretches at

a time—a school year or two here and there—was an economic necessity, no one ever told us or let us know. But it probably would not have bothered us very much if they had. We liked being there so much.

In our life, Grandfather's house was big, rambling, cool in summer and cozily warm in the winter. Mother could remember when there had been just two "ells." The front one became the parlor, the entrance hall, and the front bedrooms. Then Grandfather had built himself a library on one side and Grandmother had demanded equal space on the east, and got more because of the bay. There was a kind of big center hall—a neutral ground between where the old dining room had been and the back ell had been built on. Now this center hall was separated from Grandmother's sitting room by solid round yellow-oak pillars, and from Grandfather's library by a solid paneled door, closed only at times of crisis.

The dining room was tacked on the back, with a side porch for good measure. The kitchen was a lean-to on the back of the dining room and the summer kitchen a lean-to on the lean-to.

The upstairs had been remodeled several times, the last time being after the fire when the squirrels had almost burned the house down. Grandfather kept barrels of hickory nuts and black walnuts in the attic, and some way the squirrels discovered the loot. They made their way in under the eaves, and Grandmother heard them rolling nuts around on the attic floor over her head at night. Scoot wouldn't have stood for it, not for a minute, but he was dead by this time. Grandmother wanted to have Jay Bergstresser come to fix the eaves, but Grandfather said if "the little fellows" were sharp enough to find the nuts they could help themselves. He had more than he wanted anyway.

Then one morning when the snow was knee-deep, Carl Sigler went by on his way to church. He was Sunday School superintendent and had to be there early. He looked up and saw the whole roof of our house blazing. The "little fellows" had gnawed the wrapping off the light wires and set sparks flying in the attic. Carl yelled, and pounded on the door. Grandmother woke up and quickly directed Carl to carry out the old horsehair trunk that had all of Bobby's keepsakes in it and was stored in the front closet under the stairs for just such an emergency. Then she woke the rest of us, and Carl went and got Clarence Reynolds and Harry Watson and Doctor Carpenter and both Mister Proudfoots—the senator and the furniture man—and Frank Smith, and they made a line from the library out into the snow and handed all of Grandfather's books out hand over hand. Not a one was burned—man or book. The whole second floor went, though, and Grandfather had to have it rebuilt. Ever after that the stairs and the newel posts bore telltale streaks of charcoal in their grain, and a smell of smoke lingered in the front hall for ever so long.

The time before that when the house was remodeled was when Uncle Bobby died. This was before my time, but Mother told me.

Uncle Bobby was very much like Grandfather, with blond wavy hair and very white skin. There was a plaster copy of the Discus Thrower out in the hall on the table, and Mother said it was true that Uncle Bobby could have been the model for it.

As a matter of fact, Bobby did excel at track events and did throw the discus. He had an accident once and the disk slipped out of his hand and almost sliced his ear off. He hurried home and made the front door just as Mother was coming down the stairs. Mother took one horrified look at the blood streaming down the side of Bobby's head and fainted dead away on the hall rug. When Uncle Bobby saw Mother buckle under, he swooned on the bottom step.

Grandmother thought she heard a sound in the front of the house and came in from the kitchen. When she saw two of her children lying on the floor in a pool of blood she toppled over in the doorway. Goodness knows what would have happened if Herb Perry hadn't come along just then with the mail. He looked in through the screen door, saw the three of them lying there, stepped over Grandmother without even taking time to put the mail pouch down, and went out to the kitchen for a dipperful of water. Being of the same family so to speak, although way-off kin, he knew what easy fainters the Browns and the Hallams always were, so before Grandmother had "come to" completely he brought Mother around with a dash of well water and told her to hold a towel up to Bobby's head while he went for Dr. Baker.

Bobby was a year or so older than Mother, and they
would have graduated together from Simpson College
in the class of 1904.

Uncle Bobby wanted to play football. Grandmother
wouldn't let him because she thought it was too danger-
ous. Then one day they needed a fill-in on the practice
squad and Uncle Bobby didn't say "No" when the
coach hollered at him on the athletic field where he was
practicing hammer throwing. He couldn't very well
say, "My mother won't let me!" So he played, and
somebody put his knee into Bobby's groin. He came
home pale and nauseated and swore Mother to secrecy. She helped him with hot water bottles and turpentine stupes, but finally he started running a fever
and Grandmother found out. She took him to Denver
to see doctors there, but it was no use.

After Bobby died, Grandfather had the whole top of
the house torn off and rebuilt so that Grandmother
would not keep wandering from room to room remem-
bering this and being reminded of that.

Through all of its troubles, trials, and sorrows the
old house held on to the pointed iron grill that ran
around the roof of its porch like a crown; nor did it
lose the wide-arched cornices that framed its upstairs
windows that went clear down to the floor.

Of no architectural school whatsoever, the old house
had a kind of prim dignity. Sometimes painted gray,
sometimes brown, and occasionally an extravagant
white, it stood well back from the sidewalk in a sea of
green grass. A clematis vine growing up over the west

side sheltered the porch swing, and a heroic weeping willow's swaying branches drooped in a cascade of fragile green to the yard and the alley below. Lightning had struck the old willow a dozen times, and children had swung on it for two generations, but neither the winds of winter nor the special torments of summer could wreck its profligate splendor.

Grandfather was proud of the willow and proud of his house and proud of his ability to provide his family with the comforts he loved.

"Well, Bo!" he would say when he lifted me down from the platform of the noon train the day after school was out, "it's pretty nice to be coming back to Granddad's big old house, isn't it?" And it always was.

The front door slammed and Scoot's feet scratched to get traction on the polished floor of the front hall. I dropped the wash cloth on Bun's head and ran to meet Grandfather, but stopped dead in my tracks beside the shining yellow-oak pillars. He did not see me. He did not take off his hat. He did not have the meat. A tattered shred of what must have been the Des Moines *Register* was tucked under his arm, and there was fire in his eye. He stamped through the center hall to the dining room, and dishes rattled in the sideboard and glass chimed in the china cabinet as he crashed on to the kitchen.

I turned and followed close on his heels. Grandmother took one look at him and kept silent. He picked up the water bucket and went out to the pump under the walnut tree. Usually he threw whatever water was left in the bucket gently over Grandmother's find stand of golden-glow. Today he whooshed the stale water out into the yard, fairly drowning our new quadrille of hollyhock ladies. The pump began to protest as he churned the handle up and down with vicious vigor. Cold, clear well water ran out over the top of the bucket and splashed onto his shoes.

I whispered to Grandmother, "What's the matter?"

She shook her head but didn't look up from where she was bent over in front of the oven.

Grandfather picked up the bucket by the handle and came back into the kitchen. He set the bucket down so hard on the stool that water sloshed out onto the floor. Grandmother signaled to me to put the hot plates and the platter of mush on the table.

Bun came in, the wash cloth still sitting jauntily on her head, and slid up onto her chair. I tried to motion to her about the wash cloth, but she could not take her eyes off Grandfather. She had never seen him like this before. No one spoke, and Grandmother served the plates and passed the beets and watermelon pickle. Grandfather ate heartily, wiped his mustache on the napkin, and straightened up to look at Grandmother.

"Before you ask me do I want a piece of hot apple pie, I do. I would also like some hot coffee." Grandmother jumped up like she was shot. "Let Bo get it!" he said sharply. "I have something to say to you."

Grandmother sat down quickly, and for the first time she began to look worried. She was used to his moods and took them in her stride, but this was different.

"I want you to mark my words," he said to Grandmother as I took his plate to the kitchen. Like many
people who are hard of hearing he considered anyone
out of sight as being out of hearing. "Doc Mullican
is a malicious, minnie-brained, meddling jackass, and
you will live to see me prove it!"

"Oh!" Grandmother almost wilted with relief. It
had looked serious for a moment.

"Doc says that mule-faced college professor, Wood-
row Wilson, is keeping us out of war!" He glared at
Grandmother.

"Well, now, Papa," Grandmother said, the color
coming back to her cheeks, "you know how Doc is."

"Certainly I know how Doc is! He is a two-headed
Irish fool. Wilson is keeping us out of war! As though
we had any intention of going to war! Wilson keeps the
sun in the sky as though God had turned the whole running of the universe over to the Democrats. Orion
shines overhead at night as a gesture of munificence on
the part of Mr. T. W. Wilson and L. R. Mullican,
Dentist."

"Oh, now Papa! Doc doesn't go that far!" Unlike
the rest of us, she did not have to shout to make him
hear.

"A college teacher—a history professor! From
Princeton, of all places! How would you like to have
Professor Barrows running this country right now?"

"Professor Barrows is in the music department,"
Grandmother said with a faint smile. Grandfather did

not see it. He was attacking the flaky crust of the apple pie as though it had been made of concrete and pasteboard. The thought of Professor Barrows running the country at any time at all was so outlandish that I giggled. Grandfather did not hear me, and Grandmother shook her head at me without raising her eyes. Bun started to cry, slid out of her chair onto the floor, and crawled on her hands and knees back to the certain comfort of Benny Clayton's war.

"Surely not even Doc would think we'd get into it," Grandmother said, motioning to me to bring more coffee.

"Doc doesn't even wait for the mail to be sorted. He stands right there by the stamp window and says to Slim Judson, 'Slim, just hand me over my paper, will you?' And Slim does, and then right then and there Doc starts analyzing the news to anybody who will hold still and listen. By the time he gets back to the bank building he has built up a real case. Came in this morning a-shouting that the German Kaiser had declared war on Russia. Doc says chances are he'll backtrack into France. Now how in tarnation would Doc know? But he says that will bring England in and the first thing you know we'll have a world war!"

He stirred his coffee so hard it slopped out into the saucer, and then he glared at Grandmother. "Who ever heard of such a thing? Who? I ask you, who but Doc Mullican and the Democrats!"

The delicious steaming-hot pie might as well have been made of sand, gravel, and mud. "It beats the

Dutch how the Democrats will make political tinder out of the most far-fetched idea. And Doc falls for it! Just makes him look ridiculous saying Wilson will keep us out of something we have no intention of getting into in the first place. A whole ocean between us and the German Kaiser and Wilson is keeping us out of it!"

Grandmother pushed the sugar bowl out of the way of his elbow. "Well, mercy, that's nothing for you and Doc to quarrel about."

Grandfather used one of his rare cusswords, which showed as plain as anything the state of his wrath. "That's what makes it so damned silly! Doc's got sense enough to know its none of our business if the German Kaiser and the Russian Czar start calling each other names.

"Suppose Emperor Yoshihito should suddenly decide he didn't like the cut of Yuan Shih-Kai's kimona. According to Doc, the horse-faced college prof from Princeton would keep us out of that one, too!"

I was not at all sure who Emperor Yoshihito or Yuan Shih-Kai were, but they sounded as remote and exotic as a cup of missionary tea, and Grandmother did not shake her head at me when I snickered again. I got the feeling she didn't know who they were either.

"Oh, well . . ." Grandmother wiggled in her chair. She had work to do and our dinner had been late. "He's only teasing you, Papa. You know how Doc is."

"That's the trouble!" he bellowed, "I know how Doc is and I'm sick of it. Eugene Harlan has been asking me how I would like to move into the Harlan building. The offices are larger." He tossed his head like a small boy threatening to run away from home. Grandmother laughed and reached over to pat his short broad hand. "You couldn't see what was going on from the Harlan building. The only view you'd have would be Mamie's laundry hanging on the line out back of the hotel." She knew he wouldn't move and so did he, but he got up from the table as though he had every intention of signing the new lease before three o'clock. "Besides," she said over her shoulder as she started for the kitchen, "you'd miss Doc too much."

Later, while Grandmother and I were doing the dishes, we heard the dancing, breathy runs of the "Arkansas Traveler" on the new Horner Harmonica, and we knew Grandfather would not be leaving Doc Mullican alone on the second floor of the Indianola Bank Building—at least not that day he wouldn't.

So the crisis was over, we thought. Grandmother set the apple pie to cool in the pantry and I put the shining clean cornflower cups back on their hook hangers in the cupboard.

The old harmony of our life had been restored, to the tune of the "Arkansas Traveler"! If Grandfather and Doc Mullican had an occasional run-in about politics, that was just part of the pattern. And things like the assassination of an Austrian Archduke and a war going on far away couldn't ever possibly concern us.

We weren't aware that an era had ended on Sunday afternoon, June 27. But then very few American householders at the time had paid much attention to the news about that momentous assassination, and very many felt, as Grandfather did, that a "whole ocean between us and the German Kaiser" made our involvement in his war unthinkable.

The gunfire of Gavrilo Princip, the assassin, may have been heard around the world, but if you weren't listening you could hardly have been bothered by it. In Indianola we listened for the noon whistle, and didn't notice that the skies of the world were darkening, for the sun shone through the leaves of the trees on the courthouse lawn just as brightly golden as ever.

2

THE SQUARE

Indianola, Iowa, is not greatly different from thousands of other towns, north and south, east and west, built around a square.

The county courthouse stands in the middle of a

green lawn. The towering old gray brick structures of Grandfather's day have given way to glass-bricked, ranch-type public buildings with escalators to the courtrooms and hot air hand driers in the washrooms. There are automobiles parked around the curbing now, standing machine-mute where horses used to stomp and shake the flies away and rattle the rings of their harness and exchange bits of horse gossip about the nature of things down Milo or New Virginia way.

There used to be shade trees on the lawn, and benches too, where shaggy dogs scratched at elusive fleas and old men only paused in their purposeless whittling to bat at the flies occasionally. In those days —or what might be called the "equity period" of jurisprudence—the courthouse was three stories tall, not counting the cupola, and there were great, long steps up the north and south sides leading to the matching double doors.

The clock in the cupola had four faces, one for each side of the square. You could look out the door of C. W. Zarley's photography shop and art studio and see the time as easily as you could from Colling's Clothing Store on the east side. The four-faced clock towered above the spreading branches of the maples and the elms that sheltered the old men and the shepherd dogs, the fleas, the flies, and the hickory shavings.

Most everybody in Warren County shopped or marketed in Indianola. Some people did go to Des Moines now and then, but it was an all-day trip and the Rock Island up and back was slow and sooty, so unless your errand was mighty important it was easier and a lot cheaper to shop in Indianola.

The biggest hardware store was across the street from the bank building where Grandfather had his office. It smelled of grain and oil and shellac and red paint and turpentine. They sold lanterns and lawn furniture, and you could always tell when it would soon be spring because bright red, gleaming harrows and hay rakes began to appear on the sidewalk alongside the hardware store. Lawnmowers painted green, and big round bales of fencing wire set up bright and shining on their ends, and then, after the rains had stopped, bushels of seed onions appeared along the sidewalk in front of the store, and later tomato plants in flats. These were for the townspeople mostly. From here a blind man could have followed his own way around the square, led by his nose. Each store had its distinct and distinctive smell.

There was a German who kept a bakery right near the hardware store and his bread was considered just barely good enough for an emergency. He baked long Vienna loaves with good hard crusts and German cakes with pink frosting, and ginger cookies, fat and nippy. His place smelled of yeast and dough. He did the baking and waited on customers, too, so that a little white flour came along with the purchase, which was sacked in a gay blue-and-red-striped paper bag.

And at Christmas! What joys! Pfeffernuss and springerles and fat Kris Kringle cakes full of fruit and bulging under a shiny, foreign looking Santa Claus cut from hard smooth paper and plastered on with egg white. He sometimes carried a small fir tree in one hand, pointing it straight at heaven like a Roman candle.

We traded with Mr. Zondervan more than most because Grandmother was more modern than some. There were women in Indianola who considered it a disgrace to patronize a bakery, and no one—not even Grandmother—would have tolerated serving "store bought" to company.

Just as bananas don't taste the way they used to before our highly improved shipping methods, so doughnuts made in a miracle mile untouched by human hands can't compare with Mr. Zondervan's. His were full-bodied, sturdy, indestructible, unsinkable, undigestible. And they cost a penny apiece.

Grandfather shared our daring patronage of Mr. Zondervan. He liked the flat, limp, gummy pies Mr. Zondervan produced in what he considered the American tradition. Grandmother saved her pride in her own flaky pastry by saying Grandfather only bought Zondervan's pies to get the cardboard pie plates. On these he drew pictures. He could draw William Jennings Bryan to a T and a minstrel end man with a batwing collar, but his favorite was a tough looking customer he described mysteriously as being "Wanted for Murder."

"Wouldn't want to meet him in the alley behind the woodshed at night would you, Bo?" he would ask, and then laugh until tears came to his eyes. He had certainly never seen a "customer" as tough as the one he could draw.

The drug store was right next to the bakery, and it smelled the way a drug store ought to smell—of iodine and camphor and lavender and hyssop, ipecac, tansy, sarsaparilla, camomile, witch hazel, myrrh, cascara, paregoric, laudanum, benzoin, rubber, alcohol, castor oil, and chloroform.

Mr. Adah started carrying cosmetics at a time when the use of rice powder was a sinful practice and Grandmother had reason to swear her brood to secrecy. Mr. Adah contributed to our own delinquency twenty or thirty years later by purveying lipsticks to minors. He was a man who took pride in being up to date. We protected our source just as Grandmother's generation had, and we saved our own reputations by putting on the lipstick carefully and then taking it off just as carefully on toilet paper (Kleenex had not yet come into our lives). We had the illusion that our beauty had been vastly improved, but the artful touch was undetectable.

There was certainly Merry-Ned to pay when word got out that Dorothy Mullican had been using lipstick, but this was some time later. And it was her own fault. She bragged.

Mr. Adah sold a little candy in boxes from Bunte's, but no cigarettes. No one sold cigarettes in Indianola. It was against the law. There was one tobacco store over on the corner by the hotel, but I never set foot in that place. In fact, I always scuttled by coming from the post office, my eyes on the sidewalk and my mind on my next errand. I had the impression that they sold not only tobacco (chewing and smoking) and cigars, but snuff and maybe opium in that store. If liquor or beer had been permitted in Indianola, or pool or billiards or bowling, all of these carrion of the devil might have been carried on in the tobacco store too; but since pipe tobacco, cigars, and an·occasional chew were the only legalized vices in that day at that place, the daring outcast who ran the place must have made a meager thing of it. So insignificant a living was to be made of sin in Indianola, it seems a wonder he even bothered.

Liston's stationery and book store was on the same side as the drug store. It was also my delight and my despair.

Each penny earned or gratuitous went either to Mrs. Liston or her rivals, the Harvey sisters. Mrs. Liston's smelled of paste and fresh-cut paper and ink and ledger sheets and new books just unpacked. The Harvey sisters' "Racquet Store" or "Variety Store" was less intellectual in its appeal.

Although Mrs. Liston liked me and was glad of my patronage in the line of notebooks and pencils and paper and rulers, she was a little miffed that Grandfather never bought books from her. Everyone in town knew about Grandfather's books, and almost everyone knew what he spent for them. Grandmother had made a deal with him years before that for every book he bought he was to give her an amount of money equal to the cost of the book to spend at Allie Miller's. Allie ran a jewelry store and carried a line of fine cut glass and objets d'árt. Grandmother was an objet d'arter from way back, and she and Allie would think up things we needed desperately at home well in advance of Grandfather and Brentano's.

I couldn't tell Mrs. Liston that Grandfather thought her book selections dull, mediocre, uninspired, infantile, and evidence of a declining civilization. She would have no more understood what he had said than why he had said it.

One day during a sale I found a thin gray copy of *A Sentimental Journey* in the window, marked with a lot of other thin, gray books at twenty-five cents per copy. I took it home to Grandfather, not that he did not already have a copy which he knew almost by heart, but to show him that Mrs. Liston sometimes had her moments and that I could occasionally make good use of a quarter.

His comment was that Sterne was much too good for Mrs. Liston and had got into the job lot by mistake, and that my having spent the quarter simply proved that I no longer had it and couldn't hang on to my money no matter what. He gave me the book to remember the day by, returning my quarter, and told me to go back and see if I could find *Tristam Shandy* at a bargain.

I had a feeling that Mrs. Liston and I were being put to a test, and I was determined that we should pass it. And so, with all the earnest determination of

a squirrel expecting an early winter I began a methodical search of the books scattered helter-skelter on the
sale tables.

I never did find Tristam, but I found out about
Aunt Margaret.

Mrs. Liston had a sheet music counter in the back
of the store which was dominated by copies of *Etude*
in various hues of French-style printing. There was
also a piano which was very much out of tune, out of
date, and, for a book store, out of place. The day I
began my search there was a man sitting on the piano
stool. He was playing "I picked a lemon in the garden
of love, where they say only peaches grow." He was
wearing a high celluloid collar which was so tight his
eyes bulged. He was as bald as a croquet ball at the
back of his head but he had let the front or sides, it
was hard to tell which, grow long enough to entwine
in an intricate arrangement over the desert of his pate.
He wore spectacles of the type known as "pince-nez,"
and he was simpering up at Aunt Margaret. She was
leaning prettily on the handle of her snugly buttoned-
up parasol, and her strings and ropes of tiny, colored
sea shells swung back and forth, bumping daintily
against her bosom. She didn't see me. She wouldn't
have seen me if I had been seven feet tall and blue-
and-white striped, which I was not then and am not
now, but I took no chances. Leaving Tristam to find
himself, I lit out for home and was so dazed by the
adventure I tried to give Grandfather back his quarter.
The piano-player's name, as we all found out later

(and you'll find out more in due time), was Kize. Although no one would ever admit it, Aunt Margaret had "picked him up" at the music counter. She got rid of him in a similarly unorthodox way, but this unique and, for Kize at least, unhappy experience will be disclosed in its proper sequence.

Mrs. Liston had not, poor dear, heard of the card for special occasions. If there had been such things then as birthday, get-well, get-lost, come-back, and bon-voyage cards in that day, Mrs. Liston would have come out right on top. She was just the type for them. Unhappily for Mrs. Liston, a stationery store sold stationery and people wrote sedate, carefully spelled and precisely worded letters to one another. It may be hard to believe, but even physicians once took pride in their Spencerian penmanship, and anyone could read practically anything anybody else wrote. Signatures sometimes began and ended with a flourish, but it was a readable flourish.

Letter writing was no chore but a delight, and a talent in which ladies and gentlemen took considerable pride. Illness in town meant a personal call; illness out of town prompted a letter.

Birthdays were celebrated in the privacy of the family or not at all, and anniversaries were marked with a flushed cheek, a whispered word, and secret reminiscence until the twenty-fifth or fiftieth, when everybody and his brother joined in tendering a present of plated silver or pseudo-gold and receiving a glass of grape juice punch and a piece of angel food cake in return.

After twenty-five years it was to be assumed that the marriage had been consummated on a high spiritual plane of brotherly love, and that, the children now having been born, there was no need to imply that sex per se had ever been a factor in this union. Since divorce in Indianola was practically unknown, the silver wedding anniversary celebration was more a salute to good health and longevity than to romance and compatibility, loyalty and companionship, for if you lived you were supposed to be putting up with the same man or woman you had married no matter how devilish you and everybody else knew the "other" one to be.

But getting back to Mrs. Liston, who never lived to know the joys of a get-well card with protruding tongue or tiny hot water bottle to gurgle when the friend and patient pulled the miniature cork, she did have one seasonal merchandising frenzy. This was at Christmas, when she did a good business in diaries, day books, Elsie Dinsmore, and G. A. Henty books.

Since Grandfather thought that journals should be kept in notebooks—not diaries with mandatory dates —and that Elsie Dinsmore and Rover Boys books stunted the mental growth of minors, we avoided Liston's at holiday time except to purchase a game of Old Maid or Lotto for a cousin we'd almost forgotten.

The Central Building was on the corner right next to Liston's, and although it housed the First National Bank of Indianola it was not a spot where we tarried.

Grandmother's grandfather had built the building

and started the bank. He had also helped to found the college, and he had owned some fifteen hundred acres of land in and around Warren County. His name was David Hallam, but since questions about him were firmly discouraged, we early learned not to ask them. We even made it a habit to circle the square clockwise. If you went around counterclockwise you couldn't help looking straight into the First National Bank, because the door was set catty-corner at the top of three curved steps. We had no idea what we might see in the bank, but to us it was associated in some sinister way with "the secret."

The east side of the square was a place of enchanting variety. It seemed longer than the other sides, but since it was really a square, it must have been all the fascinating windows along it that gave the east side its air of spaciousness.

There was Meek and Robertson's, and Allie Miller's jewelry store. Colling's Clothing, run by a pleasant uncle on our father's side. The Candy Kitchen, and Grandfather's tailor. The mysterious unwholesomeness of the tobacco store, and—when I was very young —Moie Sing Bo.

Moie Sing Bo could have been the model for Bret Harte's "Heathen Chinee." He wore loose-fitting pajamas and a pigtail and a round, flat kind of black hat. He talked the way a vaudeville comedian would have had him talk.

He had a little slot of a spot between two buildings

that had at one time been a weighing station. Here he ran his laundry in full sight of the street.

Moie did Grandfather's weekly shirt, and Grandfather tended to Moie's legal business, which had to do with citizenship, rents, and the yearly draft Moie sent home to China. But their association went beyond this purely professional limit. They were both early risers, preferring to start their day before the sun was up, so for many years Grandfather, crossing the deserted courthouse grounds, his way lighted only by the stars, would meet Moie coming from the one-room shack where he lived behind the jail.

Moie would beam at Grandfather and say, "Belly cold this morning, Mister Blown."

And Grandfather would answer, "If you'd tuck your shirt down into your pants, Moie, your belly wouldn't be cold."

Neither Moie nor Grandfather ever tired of this joke, and they repeated it with embellishments for years, in all seasons.

Our contact with Moie Sing Bo was chiefly through the glass window of his tiny laundry, where we could see him winter and summer raising great clouds of steam, ironing away with gusto on Grandfather's or Judge Berry's white shirts or separate collars. Grandfather always took his own shirts and brought them home again, because he liked the excuse to visit Moie. Since we were denied the pleasure of those before-dawn greetings on the courthouse lawn we contented

ourselves with learning the "Heathen Chinee" by
heart. Any political implications of Bret Harte's satire
were completely lost on us, but not, as it happened,
on Moie Sing Bo. Perhaps we would not have made
fun of his pigtail or tried to imitate him or mimic
his peculiarly tongue-tied speech, but we never really
had a chance to find out. Grandfather put a kind of
protective screen around Moie, as light as the wreath
of steam that encircled our Chinee on a winter's day,
but as formidable to us as a barbed-wire fence. Before
we were grown, our one contact with the mysterious
East shaved off his pigtail, drew out his savings,
dressed himself in a suit exactly like Grandfather's
(which was the only kind of suit the tailor knew to
cut) and caught the eastbound out of Des Moines
for Chicago.

There he set himself up as an importer of saki,
which beverage he made in the back room of a dentist
on Archer Avenue who was indeed in the opium trade.

It was during this phase of Moie's career that
Grandfather visited him one time when he was in
Chicago on Sedgwick business. They made a night of
it, eating at all the best restaurants up and down
Twenty-second Street and ending up in what Grandfather discreetly referred to as "Moie's Chapel," pea-
cock feathers and all. I don't know that Grandfather
ever visited the Joss House again, but he saw quite a
little of Moie and other members of the On Leong
Tong. He always looked forward to his Chicago trips,
especially after Moie gave up bootlegging and went

back into the laundry business, this time on a fine scale, supplying starched white uniforms to doctors, dentists, barbers, and, when occasion demanded, abortionists.

Naturally, Grandfather never did tell us all this. When asked if he had seen Moie, he would say, "Yes," and when asked how Moie was, he would say, "Fine."

We never told Grandfather *our* story either, though. How was he or anyone else to know that many years later when we had gone to Chicago to make what was hopefully referred to in Iowa as "a name for ourselves," Bun would have a beau who was frantically trying to make a name for himself, too. The name he had in mind was Steve Hannigan, but since his idol had already spoken for this name himself, Bun's beau, Larry, had to do the best he could with what was at hand. His first and for a time only client was a business men's organization generally based on Twenty-second Street, the venerable president of which was a gray-bearded, twinkly-eyed old Chinaman with long fingernails, a benign smile, a round belly, and an Iowa accent.

After Moie left Indianola the tailor shop expanded to take in the erstwhile laundry warren. Thereafter the tailor, in his shirtsleeves, sat cross-legged in the front window, basting, basting, and basting. We assumed that he was sewing on Grandfather's suits and we were pleased beyond words that he spent so much time on them. He never became one of our personal friends, though. He had a sort of Old World look about him, and he never invited us into his shop. But then he was very nearsighted, and probably could not see us going by to the Candy Kitchen.

The Candy Kitchen was a place of dim delight. Two very dark-haired, dark-skinned, dark-eyed, round-faced, jovial men whose name was something like Papanopulus sold home-made candy. They made elegant fudge and penuchi full of nuts and stomach-ache, and peanut brittle and hand-dipped fondant in good bitter chocolate that turned a bleak gray in hot weather.

There were rows of square jars with round tops along the counter, and these held horehound, anise drops, angelica, and peppermints that nobody bought except when sent especially by their grandmother.

At Christmas time the Candy Kitchen featured ribbon candy and cocoanut whirls and special taffies, flat and filled and shining, all for sixteen cents a pound.

In the summer the youth of the town were drawn to the Candy Kitchen like noisy moths, squealing and pushing and snickering, the girls ogling the boys and the boys being absolutely indifferent to the girls. Most everyone drank sarsaparilla or raspberry phosphate, but sometimes Dorothy Hopper, who nearly always had a fat purse because of her very rich Aunt Eloise, would treat all hands to a chocolate soda or even a banana split.

At first there were just round tables with curled wire chairs in the cavernous rear of the Candy Kitchen. Later there were booths where college boys could take their dates after the movie and linger awhile in the clatter of the high-ceilinged room, over which hung the tingling sweet smell of sugar burnt to caramel, and molasses brought to a boil with a dash of vinegar added.

Meek and Robertson's was a place of dreams, even visions of personal splendor—not entirely because it was a store that smelled deliciously of cambric and calico and oilcloth lengths, but also because Charlie Meek was always just inside the front door to greet you in person.

He had perfectly capable help who waited on customers, but Charlie set the mood. He knew everybody in the county and their children and grandchildren. He extended credit with such a flourish that one got the impression everything in the store was free. He advised on colors and yardage and widths and trimmings, and he cleaned up the stories the traveling salesmen told him so that they were acceptable even to Grandmother. She blushed at the risque ones, which he whispered to her when I went to look at hair ribbons. I could always tell when it was all right to come back, not because she would laugh but because she would say, "Charlie! You are a fright!" But she never said it as though she meant it, and her eyes would still be sparkling as she said, "Now Charlie, behave! We only came in for a spool of thread."

The bolts of yard goods stood just inside the door in a riot of color. Charlie would unfurl a fold of calico as though it were Lyons velvet, and snip off a sample before you could say you'd only been sent for a ring of bone buttons. These were purchased in much the same tone of voice as toilet paper. You didn't do more than ask—you never explained what for. Bone buttons were used on long underwear, down the front and across the seat flap because they were less expensive than pearl and went through the wringer better.

The trimming counter with its ribbons and buttons and thread and braids was down the left-hand wall. To reach the ready-mades you had to climb the steep, oiled stairs past the balcony where the little baskets whipped up with things to be wrapped and change to be made. Sometimes the baskets jammed on the wires and Charlie would get a long fishing pole and push them along the wire with a smile and a quip and a comment on modern inventions and how his "overhead" would ruin him yet. A great one for a pun was Charlie.

It hardly seemed right that Charlie Meek should have been the first one to be killed in an automobile on the Des Moines road. He had just learned to drive and was trying it out alone.

Years and years later his son Joe ran for United States Senator from Illinois and was defeated, but Mother said Joe's losing wasn't as important as his father's not being there to be proud of what a good race he made.

Then there was Trimble's shoe store where Grandfather sent us to be shod. It was perfectly safe to go to Mr. Trimble without an older person along, for Mr. Trimble knew exactly what was right and what you should be sold. There were rows and rows of yellow shoe boxes that smelled of new leather and shoe polish, and it didn't matter how clearly or loudly you protested that you wanted the patent leathers with the heels in the window, Mr. Trimble, wearing his neat shirtsleeves and his kind, firm smile, fitted you out in brown calf oxfords with flat heels and arch supports, all the while discoursing on posture, the virtues of walking, and the absolute necessity of maintaining good, healthy feet. Somebody must have bought the narrow pointy-toed patent leathers with the heels, but it wasn't us. Thanks to Mr. Trimble we grew up with the metatarsals of Pocahontas and the phalanges of an ape. Dr. Scholl would have starved to death if he had depended on Mr. Trimble.

Colling's Clothing Store was right next to the shoe store. Uncle Ralph, who owned the haberdashery, was a married-on, and on Father's side to boot. He stood outside the store in the shade of the awning most of the time. In good weather the awning, which reached almost to the curbing, was down to keep the sun out. In bad weather it was down to keep the rain off. It took a most unusual kind of a day to get Uncle Ralph out with the crank to grind at the gears that lifted the scalloped green-and-white awning slap up against the front of the building.

Uncle Ralph had no children—he was along in years when he married Aunt Fairie—and he was one of the childless who accepts his fate but makes the most of it by enjoying the company of the children of his friends and married-ons.

He was an extremely handsome man with black curly hair, and he invariably invited us in for a treat. Sometimes Dorothy Hopper would suggest that we circle the square just to see what Uncle Ralph had to offer. (Those were the days when riotous living had cut Aunt Eloise's generosity down to zero.)

Uncle Ralph rarely failed us. Chewing gum, sour fruit drops, some days even chocolate drops made like cones with a paraffin-like white filling, would be doled out to us in little blue-and-red-and-green-striped paper sacks.

Grandfather traded with Uncle Ralph, but Grandmother never darkened his door. "Out of loyalty to Gertrude," she said.

Gertrude, our mother, and Clyde, our father, had already set a pattern for a life of cheerful disagreement. Grandmother naturally followed her daughter's lead, and proceeded to wage her own private war against Father's family.

This never seemed to bother Uncle Ralph any, because when Grandmother was with us he would smile and say, "Good morning, Mrs. Brown." But she would sweep by with a curt nod of her head, like a Northern officer reviewing Confederate troops or vice versa.

Uncle Ralph never offered us any candy on the days we came to town with her.

Allie Miller's jewelry store was neither exciting nor fun, principally because Grandmother and Mrs. Miller talked so much. They were very good friends. Mrs. Miller and her beautiful daughter Patti, who could swallow air and belch it up again at will, lived behind us on Salem Street. Grandmother and Mrs. Miller were always running back and forth up the alley for short visits, and why they needed to take business hours for more of the same we never understood.

Nor did the glitter and shine of cut glass bowls and pitchers or the tinkle of marble clocks or the glint of plated silver impress us. We had more cut glass at home than there was room for in the china closet, more clocks than there was time to keep wound, and more silver than we could polish on a Saturday morning.

For a while we would watch the little old man peer through the little round glass on the end of his nose, fishing and poking around in the works of somebody's watch like a raccoon hunting for grubs on an old stump, but even this diversion could last just so long, and finally we would begin to shift from one foot to another and finger the little blue velvet pad used for the display of rings, until at last Grandmother would say, "I'll have to run along. I've got the meddlesome ones along with me today."

And we would start out down the steps to the post office.

3

FROM SCHIMMELPFENNIG'S
TO THE EMPRESS

Our personal mail was delivered by a friend of ours
who read all the postal cards and knew every member
of the family by his or her first name.

He was way-off kin, but had also been a childhood

playmate of Uncle Bobby's or something, because he had special knowledge of and interest in the family, and Grandmother always talked to and about him with the particular turn of inflection which she used for those in special and lasting favor. The mailman's name was Herb Perry. He sang bass in the church choir. He had heavy, coarse, simian features, but Mother was partial to him. Whenever she was at home and he brought the mail up the front walk, she would say, "Why, Herb Perry!" and smile and walk up the street with him while he delivered the mail, sometimes as far as Judge Berry's house or farther. The weather didn't matter either. Mother liked walking in the rain or the snow quite as much as most people enjoy walking in the sunshine.

When Aunt Dot, whose real name was Myrtle Monina Dott Sophia Morrow Hamilton, married George Faieth Smith and took to ranching out in Idaho, Herb was as interested as the next one, since he had known Aunt Dot all his life and had gone to school to her when she taught out at the old North School.

"What do you hear from the folks out in Idaho?" he'd ask, and Grandmother would have to tell him something since he knew she'd had a letter only yesterday. Or he would say, "Well, I see Bo has gone to visit Clyde's folks in Newton!", which he knew before Grandmother did, having read my postal card coming down the street. We used to count on Herb as a dissemination point, because he delivered mail to

Dorothy Hopper, and to the Mullicans, Carpenters, Claytons, and Siglers. Consequently, some of our messages were meant especially for Herb's eyes, and Grandmother might be mildly curious as to why she received messages like the following one on the back of a brightly colored picture of the main street of Newton, Iowa.

Dear Grandmother:
 Fairie-Mae isn't allowed to date but I had one anyway with the most deevine boy. His name isn't Maytag but his father makes washing machines just the same. I guess you can make washing machines even if your father isn't—a Maytag I mean. We went out to the country club in his Stutz. Whoopee! And had drinks. Holy Cow! I can't imagine why Mother insists upon leaving this heavenly town tomorrow. Carl and I are practically engaged! Love, Bo.

The last sentence was written around the edge of the card, but Herb twisted it around so that he got the sense of it, and sure enough when he passed Mullicans he called out to Dorothy and Martha, who were sitting on the porch, "Well, I hear Bo is going to marry a Newton boy. Yes sir, not exactly a Maytag but in the right business."

There is a convenient phrase frequently used in the newspaper business to avoid charges of libel, or simply to flush birds: "according to a reliable source," it goes, or, "according to an unimpeachable source." Herb Perry was the original "reliable source."

Grandfather would not trust his mail to the vagaries of domestic life, and kept a business box at the post office, at the center of the bottom tier. Once it had had a key or a combination, but that was long ago in some other administration, and now you could open the box with your fingernail. You could lean over and peer into it through the little glass door to see if there was any mail, but never would any of us think of opening it unless Grandfather sent us specifically for the mail. And then we would proudly carry the long legal envelopes and law journals to his office in the bank building as though they were imperial mandates and we the Emperor's couriers.

Grandmother's trips to the post office were usually for the purpose of buying stamps or mailing a package to Aunt Dot, whom she felt had gone to live in a foreign land with an utter stranger. We usually went with her, and from the post office continued around the south side of the square.

The Hotel Indianola was down East Salem, as was Keeney's Livery Stable, but we seldom went that way except to call on Madge Harlan.

Some people went to the Hotel Indianola for dinner after church, but we ate at home except on hot Sundays in summer when Grandmother didn't feel like firing up the wood stove, or when there were just three or four of us at home. But then we ate at Swartzlander's Cafe.

The Hotel Indianola was mostly for emergencies and drummers, as was Keeney's Livery Stable. Traveling salesmen tried their level best to finish up and get back to Des Moines on the night train, and rarely was one caught out over Sunday in what they called "The Holy City."

The drummers used Keeney's rigs to go down-country to Summerset, Winterset, Milo, Chariton, or New Virginia, and for this the livery stable was a great boon to trade. With so little local patronage the hotel was, in a manner of speaking, just a landmark, or a haven for the unwary stranger. The townspeople knew it was there, as they were aware of Silas Keeney's livery, and they were grateful for the availability of both conveniences, even as they prayed God they would be spared the necessity of having to use either.

Unless Madge Harlan or Bess Scroggs had produced a new baby in the past few weeks (Bess had once startled the town by producing twins long after you'd have thought she would have had done with such things), Grandmother would pick her way around the south side past Lem Swartzlander's, Schimmel-pfennig's, and Orin Peck's.

Lem Swartzlander kept a restaurant like a surgeon keeps his operating room—gleaming, spotless, fleck-less, and constantly at body temperature. In the winter the front windows steamed over until you couldn't see in or out. In the summer the big ceiling fan stirred the hot air rising from the steam tables in a lazy, murmuring maelstrom of humidity.

The walls were white tile and the tables had mar-ble tops, against which the catsup bottles and the tall pepper shakers looked like containers of fresh-let blood and iodine. There was a counter down the right side and low stools covered with black oilcloth. Over against the wall were cabinets full of apple pies that had cardboard crusts, and cocoanut cake three layers high that tasted of laundry soap, and home-made doughnuts that Grandfather considered edible only after the third day. It was probably not true that Lem had a deal with Zondervan for the left-overs, but it might as well have been.

There were slots in the wall at the back, and the waitresses hollered their orders through to the cook, who rattled iron skillets on the iron stove and made a big show of male cookery. "Burn one for Mr. Brown and keep the gravy!"

Grandfather said the reason Lem's steaks were so good was because the cook wasn't afraid to take the lids off the eyes of the fire. Grandmother never said a word, but she knew the reason Lem's steaks were so good was because he raised and butchered his own beef and surreptitiously resorted to "hanging," a process Emil Schimmelpfennig considered pagan and Grandfather would have condemned as sure invitation to cholera morbus.

Lem sat on a stool by the cash register and cigars near the front door. He always greeted us coming in and going out, and if he wasn't too busy—there being few salesmen around on Sunday—he would come over to see how everything was.

He and Grandfather had some jokes about the steak

being as tender as a woman's heart or the recollection
of a first love, but Lem always saw to it that Grandfather had things just the way he wanted them: potatoes light brown, steak thin and black, vegetables without butter, and coffee black as sin.

On the way out I always helped myself to a toothpick from the holder by the cash register and gave one
to Bun, but Grandmother made us throw them down
as soon as we were outside. We had toothpicks on
the table at home, but a toothpick in private and a
toothpick on the street were two different things. This
was a hard lesson to learn. Tooth-picking, nail-filing
or cleaning, hair-combing, comprised a domestic litany,
so it was practically impossible to skip any one of these
personal chores, but these matters were of a piece with
belching. They were proper only in privacy, and never
were they alluded to in public. Gum-chewing was not
recognized as a necessity either at home or abroad, and
was therefore frowned upon generally. Lem gave us
sticks of gum sometimes, but Grandmother made us
throw them under the bridalwreath bushes on the way
home.

There is something else you ought to know about
Lem. He was a frail looking man, small-boned and
thin, with little feet. He sat right there making change
and talking to people until, in the late thirties, he decided if he was ever going to go back to Bavaria to
visit his mother he'd better make it snappy. So he
went back. He didn't stay long, and the more he got
to thinking about Germany and Hitler the more he

talked about it. And the more he talked about Hitler the less people paid any attention to him.

Putting two and two together after Lem opened his wrists with a butcher knife, people could see how serious he had been about the forces of evil abroad in the world, but in those days Hitler had been little more than a name and Lem's obsession something of a bore.

Grandfather was on his way back from his early-morning trip to the post office the day they found Lem's body. He said blood was spattered all over the white marble everywhere.

Emil Schimmelpfennig's was on the same side as Swartzlander's. There were great meat hooks in the front window where sides of beef, lamb, or pork hung in cold weather and long strings of weiners and sausage hung when the weather turned mild.

There was a long, high meat case along one side of the room filled with hams and sides of bacon, and a meat block at the back of the shop. Emil Schimmelpfennig wore a big white canvas apron and blue sleeve-holders that ballooned his blue-and-black-striped madras shirt up around his shoulders. His felt hat made sense in the winter because the shop was as cold as a gravedigger's nose, just as Grandfather said. In the summer Emil wore a straw "sailor," well aged and yellowed, far back on his head.

Almost everything was cut to order.

"Good afternoon, Mr. Schimmelpfennig! Grandmother wants a six-pound pork roast for tomorrow."

The big, red-faced man would leave off whittling

away at the yellow suet along a great side of beef, snatch up the steel, make two or three honing passes along it with his knife, already razor sharp, and disappear into a kind of great wooden cave. The door would swing to with a resounding bang, and there would be a terrifying moment when it seemed plain that our Emil had locked himself in. We would wait, kicking the clean sawdust into little mounds with the toe of Mr. Trimble's best brown-calf oxfords. And soon Mr. Schimmelpfennig would appear with a most lifelike white pig. With sundry remarks about how Grandmother always wanted the best and farmers weren't doing as well by their pigs as they used to, he would set to work with a great flourish of cold steel to dismantle the carcass of what kept looking disturbingly like some one we had known.

In the winter, Schimmelpfennig kept an array of deep, round, straight-sided white porcelain crocks along the side wall opposite the splendid but impractical showcase. You don't see these around any more, but at one time they were commonplace. Used for salting meats, putting eggs down in waterglass, and for making sauerkraut, they were also handy for making dandelion or elder-flower wine, but this was done strictly on the Q-T.

Schimmelpfennig kept gray, oozing, shucked oysters in one crock, fluffy yellow lye hominy in another, and home-made dill pickles in brine in another. There were two kinds of kraut—the regular kind that smelled to heaven and a fancy kind that was packed into green-bell peppers.

"Grandmother should have kraut with the pork, nein?" he would ask, wrapping up the roast in brown paper. It was an idle question. Had Grandmother wanted kraut we would have said so in the first place. No one but Grandfather dared anticipate Grandmother's orders. When this did happen, Schimmelpfennig would fill a square cardboard pail with the kraut or the pickles or the oysters, clamp down the top and pull up the wire handle. Even Grandfather had trouble getting home without its dripping.

"Liver for the pussycat?" the butcher would ask, or "Bones for Scoot?" These were free and we took them along, sure that the animal in question would . be glad to see them no matter what.

Orin Peck's was on the same side of the square. Orin was way-off cousin to Grandmother and she gave him whatever trade she had for his kind of wares. This meant that our hammocks were always two seasons behind the styles. We could complain all we wanted to that Carpenter's hammock had a built-in pillow while ours had not; or that Clayton's fringe was longer; or that Everybody's hammock was green-and-white striped. Grandmother paid no attention, and would only reply as we hung up our yellow and brown job with the short fringe and the no pillow, "This is the kind of hammock Orin Peck carries."

Orin kept a harness shop, and there had been a

time when Grandfather's bill there had run into a pretty penny, but that was when we had kept a horse.

Grandfather said saddle horses, or carriages for that matter, were ostentatious and a nuisance, but actually he was deathly afraid of them, a fact he confided only to Frank Chapman. Grandmother had insisted upon a rig of her own when the time came that they could afford it. She drove with dash and vigor, holding the reins high and sitting up straight and bold, until one day on the way back from the cemetery Old Blanche got the bit in her teeth and made it home from Aunt Net's to the barn in six minutes flat. After that Grandmother lost interest and put up only token resistance when Grandfather said Clarence Hartzler, the county sheriff, had made him an offer for Blanche.

Cousin Orin featured a life-size wooden model of a Percheron stallion in his window. This wild-eyed beast had a real black-horse-hair mane and tail, and was draped ears to withers to rump by a yellow fly netting through which white ivory harness rings gleamed. Orin kept a fine collection of seeds, too. Grandmother gave him all her flower-seed business in addition to the bi-annual hammock purchase. We could spend the better part of a morning pulling bright-colored envelopes out of the racks, only to have Orin tell us that his bulk seed for cosmos or carnation pinks or verbena or zinnias was much better, and we would go home with half a dozen little sacks of seeds which consistently came up profusely and did Cousin Orin proud. The only trouble was that there were so many other things that came up unexpectedly with Orin's seeds: black-eyed susans, goldenrod, milkweed, timothy hay, alfalfa, clover red and white, radishes ditto, an occasional stalk of popcorn, sweet sorrel, dog fennel, and beggar's lice.

The Indianola *Herald* office stood on the corner looking musty, dirty, and dreary, with type fonts spilled in the front window and a cat asleep on a poster for a box supper which had been held at the Methodist church for good or bad back in September, 1911.

When Don Berry, the Judge's son, decided to become an apprentice newspaperman with an eye to becoming a publisher one day, everyone—even Grandmother, who loved Don as though he were her son—shook their heads and said Don was making a sad and serious mistake. Everyone's mistakes should be that fortunate.

In good weather, when the door stood open, you could smell printer's ink and the kerosene they used for cleaning type, and some days you could hear the click and the slam of the feeble old flat-bed press, and somehow, as dingy and dusty as it was, there was always a kind of civic pride emanating from the *Herald* office. The Des Moines *Register* might be bigger but it didn't tell the real news. You would never see in the *Register* that Charlie Dyke had got himself a new tractor, or that Byron Hopper had gone to learn how to make pipe organs in Lawrence, Kansas. Not that you needed the *Herald* to tell you what you knew already, but seeing it in print gave it substance and importance.

Clarence Reynolds, who lived right next door to us out on West Ashland Avenue, owned the hardware store on the west side, and it was to Clarence that we turned for frying pans, paring knives, and corks for home-made catsup. Clarence Reynolds also fixed gutters and furnaces. His nephew, Jay Bergstresser, was in the plumbing business. Jay had an impediment in his speech which bothered no one but Grandmother. She said that if Jay hadn't had a cleft palate he would have been United States Senator from Iowa, he had that much sense and charm. Jay was at our house almost as much as we were, shoring up the antique plumbing that rattled and thumped and leaked and dripped and ran over. Jay understood the devious routes of water lines and sewage tiles that honeycombed the old clapboard, jerry-built houses in which indoor plumbing had been an afterthought. He explained his talent and good luck in his distinctive speech by saying simply, "Hi yust yuk where hit oughtn't be and there hit is yuking hat me."

The Harvey girls kept a variety store on the west side, too. Belle was in her fifties and Jess was somewhat older. They both wore black sateen dresses buttoned up to their chins. Their black cotton aprons had deep pockets bulging with mystery. Blunt-nosed scissors dangled from strings tied to their belts.

The Harvey girls' variety store was a place of

unlimited wonder. They kept pencils and paper and tablets and crêpe paper, and paste and colored tissue for May baskets, and pressed-glass pickle dishes, and pepper and salt shakers in exciting varieties of shapes and sizes. You had to have the right size corks to put in the bottoms to keep the pepper and salt off the table, and these were always perversely breaking off and rattling around inside. Nevertheless the shakers, shaped like little chickens or Dutch boys and girls, made a very good first impression indeed.

A quarter would go a long way at Harvey's. Christmas was an exciting adventure, for a long list of the most suitable presents would come to scarcely more than a dollar and a half in this neat assemblage of wonders.

There was an interesting hazard, though, to shopping at Harvey's. Belle had fits, and at some seasons frequently. Aunt Margaret told of being in Harvey's one day when Belle had a seizure in the back of the store where they kept the tin pots and lids. Such a clatter only Aunt Margaret could describe.

After that, Bun and I always loitered long over our purchases from the Harvey girls. If Miss Belle ever felt indisposed when we were there she was able to make it back to the living quarters beyond the calico curtain, and we had to content ourselves with wondering if Miss Jessie really did shave her mustache like our father said she did.

Harvey's had another attraction, one that we could not discuss with Grandmother because it was part of her secret—one of the parts that was never talked about. All we knew was that Grandmother had once lived right there in that store, and the mysterious regions beyond the curtain had been her home. Her mother, Mrs. Minerva Hallam Hamilton, had kept a millinery store in this very place.

It was here that Grandfather had courted Grandmother, but that was about all we knew for sure. It was hard to find out anything about Grandmother's secret.

There were several grocery stores in Indianola and Grandfather ran an account at all of them for business reasons, but Grandmother gave most of her business to Anderson-Pearlie's. One reason was that Mrs. Pearlie belonged to Alonaidni and so did Mrs. Anderson. And both the Pearlies and the Andersons were members of the Bible Club.

We liked Anderson and Pearlie's because they gave us big, striped sacks of candy every time Grandfather paid his bill. Besides, they had the greenest bananas in town hanging upside down on great stalks in the window. We liked green bananas. You can't get bananas like that any more.

Anderson-Pearlie's was a big store with rows of japanned black canisters decorated with gold scrolls and oriental figures. Coffee was ground right before your eyes in a big funnel-shaped hopper. A couple of turns on the great, red wheel and the smell of fresh-ground coffee filled the big room as the scoop, which held three full pounds, filled up to the brim.

There were bushels of apples and dried peaches and prunes sitting around, and Mr. Anderson, who was round and red-faced, or Mr. Pearlie, who was lean and white-faced, would say, "Help yourself. Have some."

The season of Advent began with a show of citron heavy with crystallized sugar and cherries sticky with juice. All sorts of pre-Christmas extravagances came out on the counter, and Mr. Pearlie said, "Tell your Grandmother the citron's come in if she wants any for her fruit cakes."

The brooms, mops, wash baskets, clothes lines, and stepladders were stacked at the back with scrub brushes and shining galvanized pails.

The side wall had coal-oil lamps and wicks and chimneys, but since Grandfather's house had been one of the first in town to be wired for electricity we didn't have to bother with lamps.

On the other side of the store was a small-scale house furnishings department with linoleum standing in tight, crisp rolls along the side of the wall, small scatter rugs stacked like pancakes, and curtain material draped temptingly over wire holders. They carried a limited line of yard goods, and trimming and braid and a few buttons and ribbons. Grandmother said she liked Anderson and Pearlie's for patterns, but preferred Charlie Meek's for yard goods. The reason was easy to see. While Grandmother liked the Anderson and Pearlie salesgirls they were not Charlie Meek. They could measure and cut with accuracy but they could not unfurl a length of calico paisley as though it were the gossamer veiling of Araby.

Mr. Zarley kept the photographic studio next door, and here we had our pictures taken periodically against a mystic misty background of gray forests and sawed-off Ionic columns. Mr. Zarley had marked the course of solemn events relentlessly from generation to generation. There was the picture of Uncle Bobby with Herb Perry and Don Berry in their track sweaters, and Mother's old beau, Bert Kennedy, in football uniform, and Mother in her cap and gown. For the one of me in my christening dress they had made poor Mr. Zarley come away out to the house. He had focused on the bust of Beethoven on the piano and the flash pan had caused me to respond with violence, so the picture looks more like a picture of a plaster man in a baby's long lace dress than anything else at all, but Zarley doubtless did the best he could.

The photographic shop smelled mysteriously of chemicals and developing fluids, and although we only went there professionally on state occasions to mark the flying years, we felt that Mr. Zarley knew us intimately, so we would always stop and look at the pictures in his windows to see how many customers we could identify among his more recent works.

The Empress Theater was on the corner. There were two billboards standing close up to the building on either side of the ticket window. One advertised the week's attraction, the other the newest edition of the current serial. At first the man who ran the Empress had a hard time of it. Methodists took a dim view of the "living pictures," and so when they had first come to town all the nice people looked the other way when they passed the Empress.

Grandfather liked the idea of the picture show from the very first. It made no difference to him if some of the church people felt it was a cesspool of the devil. He found the pictures exciting, relaxing, and altogether satisfactory. The strict doctrines of the Methodist church bothered him not at all. His was the relaxed and effortless point of view that comes from generations of familiarity with a certain way of life. There are rich people who have this same attitude toward money. Because their father and their father's father and their father's father's father were able to afford anything they wanted, money to these singularly few Americans is neither a means nor an end nor an issue. It is to them a settled fact of life, like fresh air or tulips or robins or drinking water. There is nothing in any of these things to engage one in a lengthy explanation—an offhand observation just about covers it. As it is with the heir to gold, so it was with Grandfather and the Methodist church. He didn't have to think about it. It just *was*.

A doughty old Irish ancestor, quite content to live in Cork and worship in the Protestant Catholic church, or what Grandfather called "the English Catholic Church," was standing on the street one day when a riot broke out among some hotheads, and a pale, sickly looking minister got smashed on the head with a paving block. Despite his apparent anemia, the reverend was quite a bleeder, and he soon began to give every appearance of bleeding to death there and then.

The bystander's name was Bateman, and although he felt himself too old for any active participation in the riot, he was drawn to admire the unfortunate churchman for his courage in what was not only a one-sided fight but surely a foolhardy one. And since the good Cork man lived close by, he invited John Wesley home for a bandage, supper, and a bed.

John Wesley knew an opportunity and a likely man when he saw them, and before the night was over—in fact, almost before his bleeding stopped—he had not only converted his host into the methodical ways of the United Society, but had convinced Bateman that he was wasting his time in Cork and should, if he had a mind to save his soul, sell out, go to America, and straighten out the Colonists. Wesley even had his own ideas about where Bateman should settle to begin his missionary work. The coast of Georgia was hopeless. Wesley had tried this himself and given it up as a bad job. Nobody was ever going to impose stern self-discipline on those free-living English who had settled on the savannahs north to the settlement of Bath and south to St. Simons Island. People in and around Boston had ideas of their own. New Yorkers were too busy, but in Maryland, perhaps, a gentleman and an idea might have a chance.

That's how Grandfather's people happened to come

to America. It was also how Grandfather got off being
so casual about Methodism, which is not, if we may
say so, easy.

There were plenty of things we did not do as Methodists, but Grandfather held the view that, never having *seen* a moving picture, John Wesley could not
have condemned them, and no man could say that he
might have. So Grandfather never missed a change of
feature, and the manager so appreciated his patronage
that he put up with Scoot, who did on occasion bring
with him into the narrow, ill-ventilated theater the
pungency of the livery stable and the fragrances of the
open road.

Around the corner on West Ashland, and right next
to Orr and Proudfoot's Furniture Store and Undertaking Parlor, was the conveniently located cottage and
plot of Lundy the stonecutter.

The location of Mr. Lundy's tombstone business
seemed so apt that we never thought it unusual that
this somber business should be conducted right on the
curbing of the most fashionable street in town. On the
contrary, we considered the forest of polished red-
granite blocks and dull-gray bumpy stone obelisks as
rather decorative and artistic. Indeed, although there
was nothing even remotely free-hand about it we took
a certain pride in watching the names and dates come
to light. It is possible that Mr. Lundy was a sculptor
at heart. He did take great pride in his work and he
always kept a fine big inventory on hand.

On warm afternoons after school, when we had

made a circle of the square on an errand or on an off
chance that Uncle Ralph would see us and invite us
in, we frequently finished our tour of the square with
a small snack on Mr. Lundy's stock-in-trade. Dorothy
Hopper would get a box of crackers from Anderson-
Pearlie's and charge it to her Grandmother Buxton,
and I would supply a box of sardines which would
show up as a surprise on Grandmother's bill. One or
two of the Mullicans, usually Leota and Martha,
would join us in the fading sun as we opened the can
with the key, drained off the oil, and gingerly arranged
each sardine carefully out along the soda cracker. Then
we talked about what we planned to be when we grew
up. Leota would be an opera singer. Martha would be
a librarian or a writer. Dorothy could only be an
actress, unless she married well in the meantime.

Across the street, the long shadows of the fading
sun fingered the disheveled hair of Miss Pearl White,
depicted in the act of fighting a tiger off her heaving
bosom with nothing but her own two dainty white
hands and the hinge from the sliding door of the back
end of the Empress.

We sighed and were silent. There was a world beyond our own. But what a distant world!

When Belle Banner's cats came out, purring and
scratching their backs on the gravestones, we let them
lick the heavy Norwegian fish oil off our fingers. Then
we shivered, for the sun had gone down and we all
of us knew about Belle Banner and the lonely, cheer-
less wages of sin. We threw the empty can and the

cracker box over the fence behind Mr. Lundy's little stone-cutting house into poor Belle's delphinium bed and hurried on home as fast as we could, to be safely there before the six o'clock whistle blew.

4

MR. BROWN AND MR. WHITE

If it had not been for the local joke about Sam White being brown and O. C. Brown being white, I don't suppose it would ever have occurred to us that there was any drastic difference in the color of people.

Sam White was a handsome, tall, straight Negro with black wavy hair and a fine black mustache. He was the custodian of the Indianola Bank Building where Grandfather had his office, and the caretaker of the First Methodist church. When Grandfather went up to Des Moines or over to Chicago or out to New York or Denver, Sam took care of our furnace and shoveled our walks.

Sam must have come from somewhere, but in our lifetime he was just there, a part of our world and a part of our family connections, like Uncle Willie or Aunt Belle, only closer because in many ways we knew him better.

He had married Mattie Flummer, daughter of Old Mrs. Flummer, who did the washing for Grandmother. Mattie was a little older than Mother, and was Mother's best friend. It was Mattie who got Mother married, really—she prepared the reception, dressed the bride, and told her what she ought to know. Mattie came to help with the big family dinners on holidays and Sundays when Uncle Willie drove down from Des Moines in the Maxwell. She was the color of milk chocolate, and her face had the silent, beatific look of a Madonna.

Grandfather said Mattie made the best dumplings in the world, and only Mattie was permitted to dust in the library. Grandmother had a way of straightening up, putting books back on the shelves, and changing things around here and there. Mattie never did. She said if Mr. Brown wanted the stack of *Harper's* magazines to be on the floor in the corner, that is where they should be, and she just dusted around them. Grandfather thought there wasn't anybody in the world like Mattie, and I guess there wasn't.

Mattie's mother lived about four blocks north, at the edge of town, but not because she was segregated or anything like that. Mrs. Flummer always said she liked that location because she could have a big garden and raise chickens and have plenty of room to hang clothes. She liked to work outdoors, too, and in summer she boiled clothes in the back yard (Grandmother said she used to make her own soap before Fels-Naptha came along).

Leta White, who was Sam's daughter by his first wife, came and got the washing in a child's wagon and delivered it the same way. Off would go the sheets and the shirts and the aprons and the housedresses, tucked into a split-hickory basket under a white sheet and looking like a great loaf of bread rising for the oven. And then they would all come back again, clean and folded straight. The sheets smelled fresh of the out-of-doors, and the petticoats and housedresses and long white cotton nighties smelled of lemon verbena or lavender.

Once in a while Grandmother would be at Alonaidni when Leta brought the washing, so Bun and I would have to take the money over to Mrs. Flummer later. Or sometimes when special company was coming, like a Des Moines judge or a D.A.R. State Regent, we would be sent to Mrs. Flummer's for a dozen fresh

eggs to make an angel food. Sometimes Mattie would
bake the cake herself and we'd carry it home on a big
platter with a snowy-fresh tea towel over it.

Mrs. Flummer's house had a little picket fence
around it and a swinging gate. It had a porch where
Pa Flummer sat, but the inside of the house was the
wondrous thing. There was a green wire rack across
the front window filled to the brim with plants and
vines and shoots of things planted in tomato cans which
glistened bright and silvery in the sun. Mrs. Flummer had rose geranium and begonia and fennel and
verbena and umbrella plants and what-all. Grandmother and Mrs. Flummer were always exchanging
shoots of things for indoors.

Mrs. Flummer's house made splendid use of calen-
dars and mottoes, newspaper racks and bead curtains.
And Mrs. Flummer herself was a wizened, white-
haired, thin little gnome of a woman with no teeth
at all. We were sure she was more than a hundred
years old. It is my recollection that she had been born
in slavery or had been a slave, but we may have made
that up. She smoked a pipe, which we found utterly
charming. Pa looked like Uncle Remus, but it was a
sad disappointment to us that instead of telling us
wonderful stories about Br'er Rabbit and Br'er Fox,
all Mr. Flummer ever did was rock, spit over the edge
of the porch, and worry his hound dog with a stick.

There was another wonderful thing about Mrs.
Flummer. She could go out to the woods and come
back with leaves and ground ivy, witch hazel and

milkweed, and all sorts of strange and mysterious looking plants and sticks and roots. Then she would brew teas and tonics that would cure hiccups, trots, summer complaint, backache, or night sweats.

Hidden behind the chicken house was a small plot of ground which she referred to as the "doctorlot." "Bo," she would say, "Wait here while I go out to the doctorlot. Your grandmother will be wanting some tansy for your Aunt Maggie's trouble."

Grandmother would say, "Girls! Run over to Mrs. Flummer's and ask her for a few leaves off the rosemary in her herb garden."

But Grandfather used to say, "Yeow! This tea is bitter. Tastes like it came out of Auntie Flummer's weed patch."

It was from things like that that we learned there could be different points of view about what you might think was flatly obvious.

Why Mr. and Mrs. Flummer had come to Indianola, Iowa, I have no idea. But there they were, and then very likely Mattie would not leave her mother when she married Sam. At any rate, it was Sam who was the newcomer. Maybe the Flummers went back to the days of G. W. Carver. Carver had tried to go to school in ever so many colleges in the South and in the North, but he was not accepted until he came to Simpson College in Indianola, and that is where he got his undergraduate education. There is a Carver Hall on the campus now, but in the days of the innocent era, we were neither self-conscious nor very

knowledgeable about Carver. We had an uncle who
had been in the same chemistry class with him, but
Uncle Mort had flunked and Carver had known more
than the books, and that was about the size of it.

Mattie Flummer had worked pretty steady for
Grandmother before she married this Des Moines
widower, Sam White.

Sam didn't like to stop Mattie from working entirely,
but it was apparent he didn't approve too much of
her being away from home. Yet he didn't want to
leave Grandmother high and dry, so he let Leta come
over to help with the cleaning.

Now, for about two whole generations Grandfather
had been hoping someone in his family would turn out
to be musical. In Grandmother's sitting room we had a
fine upright piano that had come down from Des
Moines by way of Orr's undertaking and furniture
store. It was yellow oak, and polished until you could
see yourself in it. For winter it had a beautiful green
plush cover with little green balls of fringe all around
it, and for summer a "natural" linen cover with cat-
tails along the border. They were a little blurred
in spots, as though they were about to burst into seed.
This was no artistic fancy. It was pure accident. The
stencil had slipped under the brown stipple brush,
which I ought to know because I made the piano cover
in domestic science class as a Christmas present for
Grandmother. It was, in a manner of speaking, my
masterpiece, both artistically and "craft-wise."

Grandmother took piano lessons first. She went to

the Conservatory and there she fell in with Professor Barrows. Something came of this, but nothing musical.

Mother also took lessons, and so far as I know nothing romantic developed, but neither did anything of a musical nature.

Aunt Margaret was next, and all she did was fall in love with a certain Mr. Kize whom she met at the sheet music counter at Liston's. It was Mr. Kize who met his downfall in a Morris chair, but more about him later.

After about six years of weekly lessons and constant practice I could make a go at "Sparkling Dewdrops," "The Lost Chord," "Whispering Hope," and, strictly on my own initiative, "They Got to Quit Kicking My Dog Around."

So it was no wonder that Grandfather found Leta White the answer to his wistful yearning. Leta had a flair for music. She could literally and absolutely play anything she had ever heard, but better.

Grandfather had a victrola he had got as a premium with some furniture he had bought Grandmother after the house burned. It wasn't a victrola, really. It was a phonograph with a blue morning-glory horn, and to get around the fact that the manufacturers had stolen every conceivable "victrola" patent, they made the hole in the middle of the records about the size of a quarter. Thus we could only play the records that came with the machine, and while we might have missed one or two red seal releases of interest, the hundreds of records that had come with the prize were of such varied excitement that it really didn't matter. We had Josh Billings, and half a dozen Minstrel records, "The Erie Canal" and John Philip Sousa and "He's Just a Cousin of Mine," and others in plentiful variety. We also had some hymns and some cowboy songs and some instrumental records. Leta only had to hear them once and she could rip them off on the old upright with a kind of lilt and dash that would have startled their composers no end.

Grandfather hurried home from the office on the days when Leta was there, and while Grandmother fried the round steak and potatoes he sat in the rocking chair, tapping his foot, nodding his head, and watching Leta's long, thin, brown fingers gallop over the keys.

Leta grew to be very tall, and about the time she graduated from high school Grandfather had a windfall in the way of a legal fee, so he and several other men in town made it possible for Leta to go on to the Conservatory at Simpson. When she finished there (I must say we thought they ruined her musicianship completely, but the school thought differently and graduated her *summa cum laude* or something) she went to Chicago to study and to teach music in the public schools there. The last time I saw her she had come back to Indianola to visit her father. Her husband was with her. He was a very nice looking man, a little on the rotund side. He wore a beautiful tailored brown suit and his shirt and tie reflected Chicago haberdashery, but not too much so. Leta wore a broad-brimmed

hat with tulle trimming, and her fine broadcloth suit
was in the latest fashion. Grandmother was so pleased
that Leta had brought her husband to call that she
had us hurry with a tea tray (and we knew from her
tone that it must be the best silver and the freshest
linen), and fortunately Mrs. Condit had just brought
over some fresh hickory-nut tea cakes that very morning.

Leta talked about Tuskegee Institute, where it seems
she was on the faculty or an advisor or trustee maybe,
and they stayed a long time and talked about Mattie
and the old days.

Mattie had died long since.

When Grandmother had discovered that Mattie was
ill, nothing would do but to get her up to Des Moines
to see Doctor Glomquist, who was Grandmother's
doctor. Poor Sam was so worried and upset he let
Grandmother do whatever she thought best. Aunt Margaret hadn't married Uncle George yet, so she stayed
home with us and Grandmother went up to Methodist
Hospital with Mattie to be sure she got the right kind
of attention. She even sold the surgeon on letting her
go right into the operating room. If Grandfather had
been there he wouldn't have let her, because of our being a family of fainters, but he wasn't there. He was
at home trying to explain to Sam that these things happened every day. After the operation Grandmother
started talking about plans to take Mattie to the
Mayo Clinic in Rochester, but she knew it was hopeless.
Mattie was "riddled" with cancer.

They brought her back to Indianola to die, and since Mrs. Flummer was an old, old lady and Leta still a flighty kid Grandmother decided that Mattie should come to our house where we could all take care of her. But Mattie said she'd rather die at home with her folks around her, and Grandfather told Grandmother that was right. He said there was a dignity to death that everybody was entitled to. Grandmother didn't know what he meant by that and kept saying, "But Papa. We *are* Mattie's folks!" Then Grandfather said, "She means her own people." And Grandmother looked at him like he was crazy.

Each morning as soon as she got her dishes done and the beds made, Grandmother went over to sit with Mattie. She brought her soup and custards and all the tempting things she could think of that Mattie had ever liked.

The summer Mattie died wasn't much of a summer for any of us. Grandmother felt she had lost a one-sided battle with the devil, and defeat to her was an affront. Sam was inconsolable and silent and joined the Methodist church.

Afterward, Grandfather would sometimes say suddenly, at the table, "These biscuits are good, but not like the ones Mattie used to make." And then one of us would get the sniffles and leave the table and Grandfather would shout at Grandmother, "What's the matter with *her*?"

Mattie's going had a most unusual effect on Mother. She got a kind of far-off look in her eyes and started talking about Bert Kennedy, an old beau of hers who had gone to South America to live. It seems Mattie had thought Mother should marry Bert, and had planned to help out with the elopement. At the last minute Mother got cold feet and couldn't risk Grandfather's wrath, and since our father was handy and agreeable and had momentary parental approval, she married him instead.

Mattie's death seemed to sharpen Mother's conviction that Mattie, as usual, had been right. Now Mother wandered around with her chin in the air and a dreamy look in her eyes, wondering, we knew full well, what would have happened if Mattie's ideas and machinations had prevailed. I knew one thing. Bun and I wouldn't have been there if Mother had married Bert instead. Bun insisted that *she* would have been (only as a gorgeous brunette with curly hair), but we both agreed that the chances of my having been born at all were pretty remote, since Mother and Bert would have been on their way to South America in the spring of '05.

Our feeling of rejection only contributed to the general air of devastation, and we mourned for Mattie as acutely as the grown-ups did.

Mattie was buried from the old Flummer house, and all of us went. It was a hot summer morning, so you could smell the rose geranium. Aunt Margaret sobbed all through the funeral services, and when Aunt Margaret cried it was like a heavy rain in spring. If you were any place around you got involved in it whether you wanted to or not.

Sam's next wife was a widow from Des Moines, too. She looked older than Mattie and she seemed more settled. She came to cook the holiday dinners and Sunday meals when Uncle Willie and Aunt Belle came down from Des Moines, but Grandmother always called her Mrs. White, and they conducted their mutual endeavors with pleasant formality.

When Grandfather had his stroke and had to be moved down to the library, where he lay surrounded by books—floor to ceiling—Sam White was the only person who could manage him.

Grandmother hired an orderly from the hospital but Grandfather ran him off. His speech was impaired to a point where he could say three- or four-syllable words with ease, but the simple and common phrase eluded him. He had never been profane. In fact he considered swearing the crutch of the indolent and unimaginative. But after he was stricken in his eighty-sixth year, he would bellow so that he could be heard for blocks. "Jenny! Tell Sam White to bring me that goddamnin-convenience!" And Sam, like a tender genie, would appear with the bedpan.

Sam shaved him, bathed him, rolled him over in bed, and gave him the news and the town gossip. When the windows were open in the summertime you could hear them laughing hilariously over some anecdote in which a fellow townsman had been justifiably embarrassed or some rascal of mutual acquaintance had got his come-uppance.

When winter came, Sam would make a second trip through the snow about ten o'clock to be sure the furnace was banked for the night. No one but Sam and Grandfather knew how to run that furnace. It was a monster of iron with curled tin tubes like arms that poked up into the floor above its head. Grandfather had always filled the bin in the fall with chunks of coal as big as a man's head. The men who delivered the coal had to be careful not to let any coal fall on "Billie," Grandfather's pet toad. Sam liked Billie, too, and was careful not to step on him when he fixed the fire. If toads grow to great age like Auntie Flummer said they did—and she knew things not found in books —then perhaps Billie is still there.

Sometimes, if it was snowy or late, Sam did not come in through the kitchen but went into the cellar through the storm door that slanted toward the house over some outdoor steps. We would know he was there because we would hear the shaking of dampers and the rattle of chains downstairs, and then we would run to stand over the registers to feel that fresh gust of hot air come billowing up, warming our petticoats and under-pants and tingling the skin along our backbone.

Then Sam would go on home the way he came. He knew that Grandmother could hear him and know that he was there, shaking the grates and fixing the dampers, and if she needed him she would call. She never went to bed until the furnace was fixed for the night anyway.

Then came the night when she needed him desperately, and Sam sat all night with his great, strong arm under Grandfather's shoulders so he could get his breath. And then he held him on into the morning until the doctor came, hoping all the time that what he felt wasn't true. But it was, and then Grandmother needed Sam more than ever. So he chopped the wood and kept the garden and shoveled the snow and fixed the fire. The old house is a fraternity house now, housing, I am told, members of Sigma Alpha Epsilon. I sometimes wonder if they waken in the night to hear damper chains rattle below, and feel an eerie gust of warm air from the registers.

Grandmother followed Grandfather as soon as she could. The honorary pallbearers were judges and senators and "boys" who had gone to school with Uncle Bobby. Some of them Grandmother had taught in Sunday School. As middle-aged barbers and grocers and bankers and teachers, they had been boys to her still.

Standing at the head of the casket, his curly hair snow-white and his mustache tinged with gray, was Sam White, the senior honorary pallbearer, wearing one of the tailored "ivy league" suits he had inherited from Grandfather, a white shirt with separate collar, and a black string tie.

A brown man named White working for a white man named Brown may not have been usual, even in Iowa. It seems to me that Ripley mentioned this fact in

one of his Believe-It-Or-Nots during his lifetime, along
with the fact that Hemphill and Turnipseed kept an
elevator and seed store there in Winterset or Summerset.

However, the friendship of these two families was
not a phenomenon singular to a town that had welcomed George Washington Carver as a student. As
facts they were totally unrelated. "Segregation" and
"integration" were words we did not know. We did
not argue issues of race, creed, and color because
there were none. Nor was this acceptance of difference
peculiar to little towns in Iowa.

We lived for a time in Morningside, which is a suburb of Sioux City, population a steady eighty-five thousand, give or take a couple. Morningside is the home
of Morningside College, a small Methodist school
similar to Simpson College in Indianola. In Iowa almost any town of any size at all has a college of some
denomination or other. There is Parsons at Fairfield,
Luther at Decorah, Grinnell at Grinnell, and Iowa
Wesleyan at Mount Pleasant. Storm Lake has Buena
Vista. Pella has Central. Coe is at Cedar Rapids and
Clarke at Dubuque. There is a Cornell College at
Mount Vernon. Drake is at Des Moines. Iowa State
at Ames is not at all the same as the University of
Iowa, which is at Iowa City. Le Mars has Westmar
and Oskaloosa is proud of William Penn. Then there
is Wartburg at Waverly. If you don't go to college in
Iowa it is your own fault.

There was an experiment in modern education going

on right across the street from Morningside College in
the institution of a Junior High School, and we went
there.

One of the girls in our class was Iona Coates. Iona
was big and soft-spoken and about the color of cocoa.
She had an almond-shaped head over which her thin
fuzzy hair was stretched in a maze of diminutive
braids. She kept safety pins and gym-shoe laces and
hairpins and court plasters in her pockets or "on" her
someway, and even the boys felt perfectly comfortable
about asking Iona for help in a crisis. This might be
anything from a lost tooth to a split in the seat of a
pair of corduroy knickers. Iona could fix a hurt or a
rip, or she could advise some modus operandi. She was
a kind of liaison officer between the faculty and us, and
she helped the domestic science teacher with the noonday lunches.

For a while we had a little assistant principal who
was about five-feet-six in his elevator shoes. Nothing
we ever did suited him, and he would bounce around
on his elevators admonishing us to be quiet or to hurry
or to go slowly or not to go at all or some equally silly
thing. He had sandy hair and wore glasses, and was
probably a young man of twenty-seven just out of
Morningside College with the ink still wet on his de-
gree. We thought of him as being at least sixty-five
years old, ancient, antique, and falling apart. But we
put up with him. There didn't seem to be much else we
could do about him, and besides he was in love with
the domestic science teacher who provided our noon-

day lunches. These consisted of the best ham salad sandwiches ever known to man, plus cup cakes and bubbling-hot chocolate. This fare, which we never did find monotonous, cost us thirty-five cents a week.

Well, anyway, there was a boy in our class by the name of Jack Rhienstrom. He was smaller than the assistant principal and he had a round, funny-looking head covered with black curly hair. His bones stuck out from his shirt as though he hadn't any skin over them, and his legs, covered with black stockings, protruded from the bottom of his corduroy knickerbockers like somber pipes. The most remarkable thing about Jack was his feet. They were the biggest feet in the class. Jack affected tennis shoes that laced clear to the toes, and this made his feet look like long black and white paddles flapping along below the wiry little bag of bones that was our friend. Jack was inclined to be original and ribald in his humor. It would seem only fair to say here and now that members of the class who have seen Jack in recent years report that he has since grown into his feet and is a man of fine stature, handsome mien, and distinguished deportment. I can only report on the boy I knew, and that happens to be Jack of the paddle feet.

On the particular day when Jack distinguished himself most especially, he said something in the front hall which the assistant principal overheard. That little man reacted with the conditioned reflexes of his calling. He reached out and caught our friend by the back of the shirt and held him aloft, dangling him off the floor so that his great, long feet churned the air about him.

Iona stepped out of line, caught the assistant principal by the back of his overcoat, and forcibly pulled him up so that his elevators barely touched the floor. For an instant they gave a kind of Chinese-gong effect, with Iona shaking the assistant principal until his glasses fell off and Jack, taking advantage of the unique situation, flaying the air with his great paddle feet as though he were out for track.

The miracle lasted for only a moment but it could have been a year, so deep and lasting was its effect on the student body. The only thing that saved it from being a catastrophe in education was the fact that the assistant principal did nothing about it. We figured and figured how come. Some thought it was because he was in love with the domestic science teacher, who needed Iona to help out with the lunches. Some were sure it was because he was ashamed to tell about being lifted off the floor that way. Some had a notion it was because Mr. Rohrem was out of town.

Silas Rohrem, who was the top man at the school, was almost always out of town. Ours was one of the first junior high schools in the country. Mother said many years later that Silas invented the junior high school, but this may have been prejudice. Mother was inclined to credit people she liked with the most amazing talents, virtues, and accomplishments, and she was very fond of Silas. At any rate, Silas Rohrem was tall and round-headed and blond, and he had the kind of a voice that can be heard in the back of an auditorium with an intimacy that seems to mean the speaker is talking only to you. No mean advantage this, especially in education. So Mr. Rohrem was kept pretty busy talking to educators and school boards all over the country, who were worried to death about the rising school population and the alarmingly increasing rate of enrollment, about our experiment in junior high-schoolism.

It was fun going to a school that Silas had anything to do with. He let us do all sorts of things that other principals would have vetoed on the spot. One time we did a modern version of *The Merchant of Venice*. Jack Rhienstrom was Shylock and I was Portia. The fact that the heroine had a lisping impediment in her speech detracted not at all from the performance— "The quality of merthy ith not thtrain'd, It droppeth ath the gentle rain from heaven upon the plathe beneath. It ith twith bleth'd: It bletheth him that givth and him that takth. 'Tith mightietht in the mightietht" —which was as effective without *s*'s as with them. So taken with their performance were the stars of this theatrical event that they decided then and there to become a banker and a lady lawyer respectively. To become actors never entered their heads.

Despite Silas Rohrem's experiment with the seventh, eighth, and ninth grades, it does not seem to me that we were atypical. While our class did include a *bona-fide* albino named Helene, of whom we were very proud, we were of a piece with hundreds of other classes in hundreds of other Iowa towns.

The state motto of Iowa is "Our Liberties We Prize and Our Rights We Will Maintain."

John L. Lewis, Harry Hopkins, Herbert Hoover, Henry Wallace, Grant Wood, Mackinlay Kantor, Keith Funston, Meredith Willson, Nathan Pusey, and Lillian Russell were all Iowans. They took the stamp of their birthplace into the world.

And so, in varying degrees, do we all.

5

JOHN WESLEY AND
THE SEVENTH DAY

There were good reasons why Indianola was known as
"The Holy City." We were a stronghold of Methodism. John Wesley would have been proud of us.

Certain things we did not do. There were disciplines
framing our way of life, and they were not to be de-
bated. We accepted them as John Wesley's method for
assuring eternal salvation.

As youngsters we were, naturally, less interested in
eternal salvation than in having a good time then and
there. However, no one asked us our opinion. Disciplines there were and that was soundly that.

We did not dance.

In a college town this is a rule of deportment that
is pretty hard to enforce. But dance we did not, even
surreptitiously. We were saved from such secret sin
as dancing might have afforded through no moral
strength, but because the girls wouldn't lead and the
boys were too self-conscious to learn.

We had "proms" at the High School and at the
College, but these were in the nature of walkathons.
We attended in pairs with our dates. On one memorable occasion a boy brought me a lovely little arrangement, something like a funeral spray in miniature, of
six sweetheart roses. This was to be worn on my shoulder to the Junior Prom.

It was not my first date, but almost, and we all
hoped fervently that Grandfather would fall asleep in
the Morris chair in the library after supper. And he
did—only to awaken the moment Ellwood touched the
doorbell. This bell was none of your new-fangled electric push-button gong-and-chime outfits. It was forth-
rightly a doorbell, with an intricately embellished
wrought-iron handle on the outside and a round iron

nipple on the inside. A good, sharp twist of the handle and you could hear the din a block away.

I was being a lady, and although I had been dressed and waiting for thirty-five minutes and had rearranged my knot of curls twenty times, I was determined to let Ellwood cool his heels awhile.

It happened all at once, like a trap springing.

Ellwood rang the bell. Grandmother ran to answer it. She slipped on the polished floor, caught herself on the newel post, then swung around and knocked a vase off the hall table, which crashed on the stairs. Ellwood got in somehow and helped Grandmother up, dropping his small funeral spray on the steps as he did.

Grandfather could always hear anything that Grandmother did, so he leaped to his feet, springing the Morris chair straight up, and started for the kitchen, where he naturally assumed Grandmother would be. In the dining room he met Mother, who was wiping her hands on a dish towel. Grandfather shouted that he would like to know what in hell was the matter.

Mother tried to keep him from reversing his direction and starting for the front hall, so she caught him by the sleeve of his shirt and tried to whisper that I had a date.

"She has a *what?*" he roared.

"A date . . . an engagement . . . a dance!" Mother whispered in a loud shout.

Grandfather looked at Mother thunderstruck. "You're crazy!" he hollered back. "Bo is a baby!"

Long before this indelicate reference to my age re-

sounded through the hall, I had started down the stairs
at top speed, letting my elegant curls flounce as they
would. But my newly-acquired high heels weren't built
for speed, and one of them propelled me into a somer-
sault that no sane acrobat would even try. I landed flat
on my face in the hall, splitting the skin on my lower
lip and all but breaking off a thumb.

Sensing now that the coast was clear to the library,
Grandmother ran into Grandfather's bathroom to get
some towels and cold water.

Ellwood and I stood in the hall facing each other.
He was as white as a sheep and I was bleeding like a
stuck pig.

In the comparative silence which followed, Grandfather's bellow could be heard from the dining room.

"Who with?"

"Ellwood Harkinstall!" Mother whispered.

"Who?" Grandfather bellowed back. "Harkinstall!
Well, for the love of Mike. His old man steals from
widow ladies and fatherless orphans."

I got Ellwood out into the night long before Grandmother came back to staunch my flowing blood. We
made it over to Mrs. Carpenter's, and she patched me
up. I didn't have to explain to Mrs. Carpenter. She
knew Grandfather. But as for Ellwood Harkinstall, he
never asked me for a date again.

Of course, the word "prom" implies walking: "A
walk for amusement or exercise, or as part of a formal or social entertainment," is the way "promenade"
is described in dictionaries. We added an orchestra

from the Conservatory and had cards to be filled out, just as for a dance. When the music started we grandmarched around the room until the music stopped, and then we went to sit with our partner until the next round.

Sometimes we had a caller brought in from Milo or Chariton, where less pious folk sometimes held dances on new barn floors or in big haymows in the spring. He would call square figures in which we might all join—but sedately. None of this bounding up and down or shaking feet or skirts or seats. We walked an allemande left and an allemande right all around the room, and then we wheeled our partner. It is surprising what a lot of rubbing-up-against with resultant afterglow you can get from this sort of thing. Dancing keeps you busy doing it right and lightly, but walking gives you more time to think.

These proms resulted in picnics which would have made John Wesley reconsider his methods. A picnic was usually held in broad daylight (sometimes at twilight, but for seniors only). The girls packed hampers of fried chicken and angel food cake and deviled eggs and pickled beets. Each girl took along enough for a family of six who had been starving with the Armenians since before the Crimean War.

When we got to Pheiffer's Woods, the boys spread out the blankets and built a fire. Nobody used the fire for anything. It was just the idea. Each boy put his blanket at a strategic distance from every other boy's blanket, so that the conversation on one blanket could

not be heard by the occupants of the next one, no matter how loud it might become at times.

There is nothing that can be done at a dance—any
dance—that approaches the opportunities of even the
first maneuver on a blanket at a picnic. In a way it
might be said that whatever the things were that John
Wesley tried to discourage by frowning on dancing
could be done quicker and (according to your point of
view) better at a picnic.

Later on, of course, the college authorities caught
on to the idea that maybe John Wesley hadn't meant
his admonition for college students when he said what
he did about dancing. But the damage was done, so far
as I was concerned. To this day the very mention of a
picnic, even a Sunday School picnic, gives me a kind of
inner trauma. Picnics and haymows have for me the
same fascination other people feel when they look down
from high buildings or see water flowing under a
bridge; the only thing I ever got at a picnic was ants,
and the only thing I ever found in a haymow was eggs.
That's the way it is with me.

Another thing John Wesley found intolerable was
the drinking of spirituous beverages. No liquor, wine,
or beer was ever sold in Indianola—then, now, or ever
shall be. Drug stores sold whatever whisky was to be
had, by prescription only.

Somehow, Grandmother always had a pint of bourbon in the medicine cabinet. It was buried way back behind the epsom salts, castor oil, vermifuge, and cas-
toria. And if, as happens to girls in their early teens,

one of us complained of cramps, Grandmother dug out the "tonic" bottle. This was hundred-proof, aged-in-the-wood, bonded-in-bond bourbon whisky. Grandmother was inclined to be as generous with her medicinal administrations as she was with butter in the cherry cobbler.

She had a little red and white glass tumbler brought back by hand from the 1876 Centennial Exposition in Philadelphia, and this she used exclusively for "tonic" administrations. First she put two teaspoonfuls of sugar in the bottom of the glass. Then she poured in two to four ounces of bonded bourbon. Filling the glass with hot water, she stirred briskly. Fortunately for us we were already lying down.

There was a black leather couch in Grandmother's sitting room, tufted with hard black buttons and sloping up at the end to make an elevation for your head right over the hot-air register.

The stricken one would be lying on this couch, covered with a hand-knitted wool afghan that had come out in the wagon. On the wall above the couch hung a heroic steel engraving of Christians about to be eaten to the marrow by ferocious and alarmingly well-fed lions of both sexes.

Grandmother would raise the head of the patient just enough for her to drink the "tonic," which she was to do all at one gulp. Immediately the lions would begin to move and the Christians begin to writhe. Before the horrible denouement of this tableau could be played to its bloody and inevitable end, the patient was mercifully consigned to the sleep of the godly. Several hours later she revived with a where-am-I feeling, absolutely cured of her ailment, a little pale around the gills, and without much mind for supper.

Grandmother would explain this lack of appetite to Grandfather in the sotto-voce shout she reserved for extremely personal matters. "She's all right, Papa, it's just her 'time'!"

We had another brush with alcohol in the person of Dr. Taylor, who was courting Aunt Margaret.

Dr. Taylor never had a first name so far as we knew, but we were all for him none the less. He was, we firmly believe to this day, the best country doctor of any place at any time. We loved him and so did everybody in Milo, where he practiced. He wanted to marry Aunt Margaret, and we certainly thought he should, but she had an idea he was a little too old for her. We thought he was absolutely fascinating. He told Grandmother risque jokes that made her blush, and he teased Grandfather about the Republicans, which was no laughing matter. He was a man of the world if ever there was one. He smoked cigars (but never in the house). He drove a Reo roadster, and he dressed for it in a tan-colored pure linen duster and cap with green goggles. He also talked out of the corner of his mouth in a wonderfully deep bass voice, and he smelled deliciously of chloroform, lysol, tobacco, sen-sen, and gasoline.

He brought bottles of wine to the house when he came to call on Sunday afternoons.

Grandmother was so anxious for Aunt Margaret to marry Dr. Taylor that she didn't dare to tell him he couldn't bring the wine. So about four o'clock on Sundays they would pull down all the shades in the dining room and close all the doors, even in August, and closing doors and windows in Iowa in August is something you don't do without good reason. Then they would open the slender, tapering bottle of sauterne, or claret—never anything as daring as champagne—and sip delicately from cut glass punch cups.

The way I found out about this was that one Sunday afternoon I came clattering into the library after having spent ten minutes of the afternoon listening to Helen Sigler play the harp, as I said I was going to do, and the rest of the time at Mrs. Burns's doing something that we were forbidden to do any day in the week but which a lot of pious people, including our sweet old neighbor, thought proper even for Sundays.

Grandfather was reading a book by the west window.

I said, "Where is everybody?"

He said, "Out in the dining room drinking wine."

If he had said, "Out in the back yard with all their clothes off," I couldn't have been more surprised.

"Drinking wine!" I hollered at him.

"Not so loud!" he said, looking at me over the rim of his glasses. These were steel-rimmed specs he got at the ten-cent store in Des Moines. He just went there and kept trying them on until he could see as far as the candy counter. And then he bought several pairs because he was always leaving them at the office or up in court or somewhere.

"Drinking wine?" I mouthed at him softly.

"They don't think I know it," he said. "And you aren't supposed to, either."

I spent the rest of the afternoon swinging on the willow tree trying to see into the dining room and telling Bun I knew something she didn't know. Both activities were frustratingly futile. The blinds were pulled down so tight you couldn't even see the window sash, and Bun didn't care what I knew.

It was several Sundays later that I accidentally came into the kitchen and caught the wine bibbers red-handed. Nobody had to tell me not to tell. I knew a secret when I saw one.

Another thing we couldn't do was play cards. We could play Old Maid, Rook, Flinch (which is still a very good game indeed), and Lotto, but not real cards.

However, Grandmother played cards, just like she wore silk stockings—unpublicly. Not clandestinely, nor surreptiously, nor secretly, but in a sense privately. If these things had hurt her conscience she would not have done them at all, but since they would have offended others she did not flaunt them.

Grandfather said she needed to do these things, that they gave her assurance that she had descended from Virginia gentlemen. He said that part of the trouble with people was they did not allow themselves the luxury of bolstering their own egos now and then.

Goodness knows he never had this trouble. He never
did play cards himself, but it wasn't because he was
taking sides between John Wesley and Grandmother,
it was just that cards bored him. He played dominoes
with Bun and me sometimes, but games were not for
him. And it wasn't much fun to play with him because
you always had to let him win. He usually did anyway,
but if he lost a couple right away he remembered something he had to do that demanded his immediate
attention.

Almost every Saturday night there was a card game
going on in the parlor, and I was so ashamed of this
defection that when I had a date for the picture show
on Saturday I said goodnight to him on the porch and
wouldn't let him into the house, on the excuse that
Grandfather was asleep.

This was usually true enough. Grandfather would
be sleeping in the library, and just the mention of
Grandfather's name was scary enough to send almost any swain kiting up the street in nothing flat.
New boys in town who hadn't gotten word about
Grandfather sometimes had to learn the hard way.
Bun said she never did have a date she didn't surprise
by jumping out from behind the old maple tree with
a casual, "I was just observing the ways of the locust,"
just as he turned in the front walk, or by leaping off
the front steps into the amazed young man's arms just
as he politely approached the bell. There was one boy,
though, who was a stranger in town. He walked Bun
home from a football game. Bun, too charmed to be

warned by the waning light, sat down on the porch
railing and so did he, with his back to the street. In
one dreadful moment the six o'clock whistle let go,
and over the new boy's shoulder Bun saw Grandfather,
the meat for supper, the evening paper, and Scoot
about even with Brewer's hitching block and Carpenter's pine tree. She grabbed the new boy by the lapels
of his coat, yanked him into the house, propelled him
through the front hall, pushed him through the big
center hall, pulled him around the dining room table,
and thrust him out the back door toward the pump
stand, saying into his stunned and beardless face, "I'll
explain later—tomorrow maybe!" She never had a
chance. He couldn't wait, so he got some of the town
boys to spell it out for him. After that he would nod
at her if they met uptown or at the picture show, but
he never smiled at her and she never got a chance to
push him through the house again.

The name of the game that occupied the attention
of Grandmother and her friends on Saturday night
was Five Hundred.

The foursome was composed, with substitutions
from time to time, of Altie Swan, Martha Burberry,
Allie Miller, and Grandmother.

Altie Swan was a Presbyterian, which made her
a comparative liberal. Tom Swan, who was her husband and about a third her size, had something to do
with farms. It seems to me that he leased or rented
hay binders or manure spreaders, or some such unlikely business. In any event, he had to work on Sat-

uɪday nights and so Altie would come down to our house. When she went home she always carried a big umbrella over her head even in the finest weather. Grandfather used to tease her about it. He said if she had been a Methodist she would have had more faith in God. She said that as a Presbyterian she had sense enough to take adequate precautions.

The problem was that Altie had to walk about four blocks under the great spreading maple trees along West Ashland Avenue. These wonderful old giants were full of squirrels who made their nests in the hollow trunks, which also harbored large families of blue jays and hooting owls. At about nine-thirty one night, when Altie was going home from Five Hundred, a young owl, swooping low, had got caught in her hair, and she had had to run in to Doc Mullican's to get it cut loose. After that, the umbrella. And no wonder.

Mrs. Miller was a widow.

Martha Burberry's husband, Sig, was a haberdasher, which accounted for his occupation on Saturday nights. So Martha came over from her house on Salem Avenue, and that made the foursome.

Grandmother figured that since they did not play for money this made it all right.

For the most part, though, we observed the rules.

Naturally, we didn't smoke.

Some real hardy customers like Doc Mullican lit up a stogie now and then. Fellows hanging around the courthouse lawn sometimes smoked a pipe.

Our father smoked cigarettes, much to the shame of

all of us but himself. He probably only did it to show off, but it had a sinister effect on us.

Once, on a hot afternoon that was to affect the remaining years of our lives, we rose from a somewhat heated family discussion of the vices to visit a matinee showing of Major Bradley's Chamber of Horrors, done uniquely and with chilling realism in wax.

Major Bradley got around the Middle-western prejudice against sensationalism by pointing morals. And he gave his dramatic talents full sway by working his nightmarish series up to a crashing climax.

The destitution of the drunkard's home was first, and bad enough, but the scene devoted to the evils of tobacco, which came next, portraying the emaciated, forsaken, jaundiced, famished, bony creature that our father was to turn into if he didn't give up the vicious habit, brought tears to our eyes. We scuttled past the opium den and its smokers, which was the last extreme of admonition, with downcast eyes. The depravity of this final exhibit was too shocking to consider even in its implications, which were, of course, that one thing led to another.

The thought of our being left in the world as ragged, sickly orphans dependent on a slatternly mother with stringy hair, while our father hid himself away in a teakwood dive in San Francisco done up in a blue-and-gold-satin kimono was just too much to bear.

The fact that our gay and irresponsible father did die at an early age had nothing whatever to do with the smoking of tobacco (as he himself with complete lack of bitterness remarked as he waited for death), much to the disappointment of a great number of people. And as for our lovely mother, adversity served to make her neater and trimmer, and the steaming heat of a kitchen at canning time only made her soft, red-brown hair curl up around her face like a baby's.

Anyway, whenever father felt the urge to indulge in a "weed," he had to go outside and sit on the porch railing, and since this was usually during the Christmas holidays, he had to bundle up in his overcoat and black bowler hat, and the smoke from his cigarette would curl away mighty faint and puny on the frosty air. His defiance seemed a tiny thing against forces so vast.

Grandfather never permitted anyone to smoke either in the house or in his office. He just ran clients off who "lit up" when they came to see him. This was the one characteristic Grandfather admired in Andrew Carnegie. Little Andy could not abide cigar smoke around, and he would go to the window and open it wide even in the coldest weather in order to hint to one of the Morgans or a Gould that smoking was frowned upon.

Otherwise, Grandfather couldn't see Andrew Carnegie with a spyglass. The library business was one he particularly frowned on. Indianola had a Carnegie Library, and Grandfather said it was the ruination of society. If there were no Carnegie libraries, people would be tempted to buy books, read books, and keep books. Grandfather said that reading a borrowed book was like wearing a borrowed coat. What

good was it? Maybe a temporary measure, but of no
lasting value. A book should remain with you, be
part of you, be there to enjoy again, to remind you of
its pleasures.

Furthermore! In the Carnegie Library a bunch of
pinch-nosed custodians of the funds picked out what
they thought you should read. This meant that everyone in Indianola should read the same thing. He
didn't intend to be dictated to by a red-nosed ex-school
teacher, so he never darkened the door of the Carnegie
Library. People were always arguing with him about
this, and he would admit that maybe free public libraries were a good thing in the poorer sections of
large cities, but by and large they destroyed initiative,
made reading a public chore instead of a private privilege, discouraged critical judgment, made learning
superficial, and took away the incentive to acquire a
personal library which everyone who had any sense
knew was the badge of the gentleman. Grandfather's
library was as personal a possession as his toothbrush,
and he was convinced that one should be as universally
owned and used as the other.

The name of Andy Carnegie was anathema to Grandfather for another reason. He had run into an assortment of "eastern" syndicates and financing schemes
while trying to keep Professor Sedgwick out of jail,
and it had suddenly occurred to him that some of the
men who sat on one board also had dealings with
other companies in which they had an interest, economic or otherwise. He thought this was downright

immoral, and when someone explained to him that Carnegie had been Pittsburgh superintendent of the Pennsylvania Railroad during the Civil War, with a salary of $2,400, while his income from corporations doing business with the railroad and the government came to over $47,000 a year, Grandfather pretty nearly had a stroke.

But Grandfather was a fair man. He often said that no man was such a scoundrel that some little good couldn't be found in him, even though sometimes only God knew what it was. If Andy did not permit smoking in his office, there was that trait to be commended, after all, no matter how black the picture looked against him in other matters.

This was not exactly the climate in which to take up smoking, especially if you happened to be a girl.

Maybe the boys were smoking out behind the barn, but we weren't—that is, we weren't until Dorothy Hopper brought her roommate home from Fairfax Hall.

Now there was a gal for you. She was spectacular then, and would be spectacular now. In the first place, she had flaming-red hair which she did in a unique and flamboyant way, sort of swirled around her head.

She talked with a deep-south accent, and she swung along like Chloe when she walked, with a kind of underslung bump. The only one of us who caught on to the secret of her walk (and we all practiced privately before the mirror for weeks) was Rosemary Mullican, who was "too young to understand what's going on," Grandmother said. Of course, this is the kind of thing that adults are always saying about children, thereby making utter fools out of the whole race of grown-ups. If there was anybody who knew exactly what she was doing it was Rosemary. Bun said that years later when she was double-dating with Rosemary up in Des Moines. They went swimming up there with a couple of boys. (This would have resulted in banishment in my day, but Bun and Rosemary grew up a decade later, when things had loosened up a bit.) Bun said when she saw Rosemary Mullican come swinging around that pool in a bathing suit she said to herself, "That girl is going places!" And she did.

To get back to the girl from Fairfax Hall, she came to visit in Indianola, and she was like the aurora borealis breaking into the dark sky when you're walking home from a prayer meeting. Grandmother said I couldn't go near the Hoppers' until after *that girl* had gone.

Every boy in town was sneaking around the back way through the alley, and then slumping 'way down on his backbone in the swing on the Hoppers' front porch so his mother couldn't see him over the porch railing.

This girl wore a skin-tight black dress. And she smoked English Ovals with a holder. Maybe they were Milo Violets, but I have a dim recollection of Dorothy's telling us later that perfumed cigarettes were "kid stuff."

Dorothy told us all this after the girl had gone—and so, unfortunately, had the boys—and the Hoppers' front porch was no longer off-limits. She was probably there only two weeks, or maybe no more than a weekend, but her impact on Indianola was so overpowering that it seemed to last all summer.

Then there was a girl in Sioux City whose name was Lois Griffin, and her brother smoked Lucky Strikes. They weren't as fashionable or exotic as Melocrinoes, English Ovals, or Milo Violets, but they were a cut above Home Runs, One-Elevens, and Piedmonts. But then, smoke is smoke.

So one day while Lois's brother was at school we went into his room, found the package of Lucky Strikes, and lit up. We were sitting quietly, puffing up a roomful of smoke—and not choking or coughing, either, as we had half-expected to in this initiation—when we heard Virgil coming up the front steps. We made a rush for the ash tray, which was setting on a stack of English One themes on his desk, but we didn't have time to crush out the cigarettes before we heard his step on the matting in the hall. Instantly Lois banged up the drop-leaf of the mahogany desk, tipping the ash tray and lacerating my eyebrow with a single motion.

As Virgil opened the door the inside of his desk was already smoldering, and wisps of smoke wafted out through its cracks and between its hinges. And standing beside it was I, a mangled mess of fresh blood and salt tears.

Virgil was a very fine fellow indeed. He strode to the desk and slapped out the fire. Then he fetched adhesive tape and pulled my wound together. Then he wiped my blood off the floor, turned the rag rug over, and promised not to tell on us. He wasn't even too upset over the charred Freshman English papers. He never did tell, but I'll carry a three-cornered scar across my eyebrow as long as I live.

Sewing was considered an admirable pastime for a girl, but it was wrong to sew on Sunday. If a button came off or a hem came out or a seam popped, in no matter how strategic a position, we could not thread a needle and tend to it.

We could not wash our hair.

We could not play games, not even Lotto, Flinch, or Rook.

We could read only those books designed to elevate our minds or improve our spiritual values.

We could look at pictures in books but we could not go to the movies. I don't even remember now whether they ran on Sunday, but probably not.

It was a variation of the picture theme that accounted for my being over at Mrs. Burns's when I should have been listening to Helen Sigler play the harp. Mrs. Burns was an old lady who lived across the street, and she had a stereoscope. Lots of people had them, but Mrs. Burns had the largest collection of pictures. Her son sent them to her from Chicago. He was in the theatrical business.

A stereoscope was a kind of visor with two lenses

in it. You cupped it to your eyes and looked through it at cards you inserted into a frame that was perched on a sliding arrangement that projected from the nose-piece. The card had twin pictures on it, but when you adjusted the frame at about a foot from your eyes you saw one picture in three dimensions.

And that was why Grandfather wouldn't have one in the house. He said if we spent all our time peering into a dark hole to look at three-dimensional nothing we would never learn to read.

So we would go over to Mrs. Burns's and look through her stereoscope. She had wonderful series: "The Wild Western Train Robbery," "The Building of the Panama Canal," "Ruins of Ancient Rome," ditto Greece, and I don't know what-all.

Bright and early every Sunday morning we had to make our beds and straighten up our rooms, but we could not do any kind of dusting, sweeping, cleaning, or scrubbing. It was all right to straighten up the small top drawers of the dresser, or to sort out the letters and things in the pigeonholes of the desk. It was *not* all right to clean out closets, the large lower drawers, attics, cellars, or wardrobe chests.

We could go for a ride, but only for no purpose. That is, we could ride in the buggy with old Ione or in the Reo with Doctor Taylor, so long as we went out to the college or over to the cemetery or out to Charlie Dyke's for no reason. If there was some purpose in all this we couldn't go.

We could not go to a party, but we could have company or be company at Sunday dinner.

We could not have dates, but we could go to the Epworth League and let the boys walk home behind us.

We had to be clean and "dressed up" for Sunday, but not too much so. That is, we were expected to wear neat, tidy, better-than-school-dresses, but never —My Lord, *never!*—did we put on a party dress for Sunday.

The Saturday-night bath routine was no joke, especially if you happened to be last and the hot-water tank was empty. But clean you must be for Sunday, with the week's dirt washed away like sins, hot or cold. Only the seriously ill had baths on Sunday, when their therapeutic value diluted the connotation of vain indulgence.

We could cook on Sunday if there was company, but we could not prepare. That is, all the wood had to be brought in for the stove on Saturday, potatoes peeled, salad jelled, pies baked, cakes frosted. Grandmother cheated a little by roasting the roast or frying the chicken or making the dumplings or the biscuits on Sunday, but for the most part we held to the rule. Grandfather said that as far as he was concerned John Wesley could have all the cold biscuits he wanted, but as for him, he'd take his newly made, freshly baked, and hot enough to melt butter.

We could also play croquet.

We could swing in the swings, hammock, or glider.

We could not do homework or study, even for a test on Monday. And no amount of tears or lamentations like, "I'll *fail*!" swerved the family point of view: "You had plenty of time on Friday night and all day Saturday. If you have not done it you will go to class unprepared!" The tearful shriek of "I forgot!" met with the stony reply, "Next time you will not forget." And, strange as it may seem to mid-century children and parents, we didn't.

We could play the piano if the piece we had in mind was solemn or classical. Since mine wasn't I couldn't, but neither could I practice, which made for a compensatory balance in that department.

We could go for walks, sometimes clear out to the fairgrounds.

We could visit, and in this way we learned a lot about conversation that we never would have learned if it hadn't been for Sundays.

The rules held for almost everyone else in town, since almost everyone else was Methodist.

One time after I was pretty well grown and in another city, a boy who had studied to become a priest and then changed his mind told me he thought that I was a pretty enough girl and that it was too bad that being a Methodist shut me forever out of Heaven. He said it wistfully, as though he had no time for giddy pursuits in this world, but had hoped to find all the pretty girls assembled in the golden streets of heavenly eternity. I pondered the lament of the young reporter-ex-seminarian for a long time, but in a way that was precisely how we looked at matters in Indianola. One could be ever so nice, jolly, and all that, but unless he or she was a Methodist he or she was not really in the swim of things. We did not, I feel sure, exclude non-Methodists from Heaven, but there was no doubt in our minds who would have the front-row seats.

We children never questioned the fact that Grandfather did not go to church. To us he was like God. He did as he pleased and no questions asked. But one day a dreadful little sharp-nosed friend of ours asked why our grandfather didn't go to church. She said it the way she was later to say to a neighbor, "What makes you think your husband is bowling every Thursday night?" Immediately on the defensive, as she intended us to be, we said Grandfather didn't go to church because he was deaf and couldn't hear. She said he could hear in court all right and that her mother said he didn't go because Grandmother wouldn't let him. Her mother said that one time Grandmother and Grandfather were coming out of the church, and just as they got to the vestibule and Grandmother was smiling and bowing and nodding to people and shaking hands with Brother Willis, Grandfather said, "That was a cracking good sermon, Willis. Too bad more of your hymn-singing, horse-stealing, mealy-mouthed, hypocritical stewards won't take it in."

The Reverend Willis went on shaking hands with Grandmother and acting like he didn't hear, so Grandfather repeated himself, only this time loud enough to be heard up on the square.

Pinch-nosed bearers of unhappy rumors are usually accurate, regrettably.

Inquiry and investigation not only proved waspy little Florence right, it opened up a wealth of information on the subject.

While Grandmother's people, the Virginians, had been members of the Episcopal church, she had easily converted herself to Grandfather's church as the obvious thing to do, and accepted the new way of life, with the exception of card-playing and the wearing of silk stockings. She had then been taken back by his casual attitude toward the whole business. "Casual" is hardly the word. He referred to the church as the United Society and he said original sin was hogwash, and that anyone who went around saying he was sanctified needed his head examined. Grandmother reminded him that his own ancestor, Irishman that he was, had been in on the Baltimore conference in 1784 that set up the Methodist church, and that this was no way to talk about his ancestor.

According to our mother, who reported that as long as she could remember Grandmother had waged a battle each Sunday morning to get him to church, this discussion of essential values had colored our grandparents' whole married life. After the event the spindle-legged Florence reported to us, we discovered that the incident was not only true but had become a legend, particularly with those members of our community whom Grandfather had defeated or bested at court. Some thought he had done it intentionally to get out of going to church. If this was the case, it had worked, for Grandmother never again insisted on his attendance at church. She continued to teach a Sunday School class and was "active" in missionary work. To make up for Grandfather's evident lack of interest, she went twice on Sundays and to Wednesday night prayer-meetings, and took me with her. She must have thought that, like a squirrel, I could store up in the summer what I needed to carry me over the winter, since Sioux City, where we lived during some of the school years, had the reputation of being "fast." Sioux City may have been, but Morningside, the suburb where we lived, was not. Morningside was Methodist and had a Methodist college.

Here Father sang in *The Messiah* and we had band concerts in Peters Park and Hartzell Spence stole white lilacs for us from the hedge at Dr. Mossman's house. We used the white lilacs for our May baskets. Dr. Mossman was president of Morningside, and Hartzell was the son of the Methodist minister.

Walking through the park one time, I heard a boy named Carl Carstensen tell a boy by the name of Doug Countermine that Eunice Adams and I were flirts.

Eunice didn't care. She went home, grew to be more beautiful, married Robert Quiette of The Theater, and went to live in London and Santiago, where her husband became associated with Paul Gregory. If she was a flirt, she was a good one.

With me it was different. I went home and cried.

But aside from that, nothing very racy went on in Sioux City except Eunice Adams' parrot.

Mr. Adams was a "commission man," which meant he traded in beef cattle. The middleman between the ranch and the slaughter-house is a "commission man." The day prohibition came into being, Mr. Adams celebrated the sad event at his favorite bar at the stockyards. When the smoke had cleared away he found himself the lucky owner of the tavern parrot.

We were enchanted to get the word from Eunice and Darrel (the latter being my first real "crush" at the age of ten) that the parrot had arrived. We were even more enchanted when we discovered that his vocabulary was what might be expected from any bird raised in the biggest saloon in the biggest stockyards between Chicago and Cheyenne.

Mrs. Adams tried to tone him down, and for a while the out-of-doors did the trick. Sitting in his cage on the stoop, he must have had the illusion of being wild in the sun again. At any rate, he tempered his conversation to the awks of the jungle, or wherever he had come from. But then came the electrifying day when there was a Ladies' Aid meeting at the church on the corner, and all the ladies came by on their way to aid the heathen, foreign and domestic. The parrot took his stance and started calling out to them. He started his greetings with "Hello, dear. Hello, dear." And then in apparent disgust, "Oh! Hell! Oh!" There followed then a barrage of good old sixteenth-century English that would have made Shakespeare sit up and take notice. That parrot must have had the largest vocabulary of any bird in America —and all bad words.

If parrots really do live to be a hundred or so, he may still be around somewhere gladdening the hearts of little children with his ribaldry. I devoutly hope so. It was such a unique and exciting way to learn one's four-letter words—having them called out by a parrot to members of the Ladies' Aid and Foreign Missionary Society. Where did you hear that! A bird told me!

Since no society is likely to be all of a piece, either in County Cork or St. Mark's Square, it is natural to suppose that there were individuals in our immediate neighborhood who did not qualify as either Protestants, Christians, or members of the Methodist church. The fact is that we found any or all of these differences as exciting and interesting and as much to be admired as Helene Morse's white hair and pink eyes or Iona Coates's chocolate skin and lacy pigtails.

As a matter of fact, people who broke away from the familiar paths were up-graded instead of down-graded in our eyes. When Mary Kirk, a Protestant, married Lawrence Davidson, a Jew, all the other girls were green with envy—not because he was as handsome as Adonis or because his father owned a department store, but because he was so excitingly romantic. Lawrence had a brother, Herman, who was in my class. I did everything I could to win Herman's heart, but he was too busy qualifying for Yale or Princeton or one of the other eastern colleges to offer me anything but friendship.

Then there were the Grabowskis and the Millers and the Rosensteins, and Wallace and Dorothy Dreyfus.

Maybe their parents knew, and maybe ours did, too, that out in the world there could be talk about tolerance and intolerance, understanding, anti-this and anti-that. If they knew, they never mentioned it, so we grew up not knowing such things. We were all friends, natural and relaxed and happy to be together. The fact that some families went to one church and others to another was a simple result of God-ordered inheritance, just as some family names were Johnson and others were Olson or Smith or Corntassel.

Years later, in the days of James Branch Cabell and *Jurgen,* Meyer Levin and I were listed on the same newspaper's payroll in Chicago. We also lived as neighbors on Wells Street. If the Middle West had a Greenwich Village, this was it. Having come from a town where, despite certain rigid rules of conduct, the dominating spirit of the people was respect for the idiosyncracies of others, I had the greatest difficulty adapting to what passed for "liberalism" in the city. I thought of myself as a provincial booby (and this was the only opinion I shared with my neighbors), but on the other hand the avant-gardes' declaration of tolerance and their studied efforts toward garish eccentricity struck me as being little more than meaningless posturing.

Meyer and I were friends, and so before he went to Palestine to raise oranges, leaving me friendless and frighteningly alone, we had a talk about the people who made up our elaborately self-conscious environment. He explained that they were the emotionally *"nouveaux riches"* who were just discovering in their own way the fun of self-expression. The reason why they baffled me was that I was raised in a community where respect for the individual was the most elementary principle of living. Meyer then predicted that the lackluster, pretentious freedoms of the twenties would develop into a regimented mediocrity by mid-century.

Growing up in Iowa, I had learned that the secret of getting along with people is to acknowledge differences—all differences—and to respect them. There was a greater-than-life-size picture painted on the side of a grain elevator in Ute, and for years we watched for it whenever we went to Grandmother's on the train. In the picture was a big monkey who had caught a cat by the tail. The cat was stretching out to catch a mouse, and the mouse was sitting up preening his whiskers (Bun says the mouse was scampering away with his tail in the air.) The painting got dimmer and dimmer with the years until at last it faded away into the gray clapboard siding of the elevator, but the printing above it is as bold and clear as it ever was: "Live and Let Live!"

When, in the days of my Chicago experience, I told Grandfather about the man who went barefoot in winter, the girl who kept a tiger as a pet, the man who dyed his long, brown beard bright red, the artist who wore ladies' straw hats summer and winter, the writer whose mistress was older than his mother, the poet who would not take a bath, etc., etc., he looked at me in astonishment. "What a pity," he said, "that there could be young people so unsure of themselves! How lonely they must be inside."

It was during these days of a double life, when my week-days were spent in Chicago and Sol Cohen's Wells Street Studios, and my weekends in Indianola with Grandfather and the Methodists, that he said to me, "God does create men equal, I feel sure, but He never said He had any intention of making them all the same!"

Grandfather was also a great one for reading the Old Testament. There were two rockers in the library, one on either side of the oval oak table. Grandfather sat in the Morris chair and read by the light from the stained-glass-shaded lamp. Grandfather had a way of giving a virility to the kings and the prophets that made them more exciting to us than characters out of Dumas or Stevenson. He would read a bit, then lay the Bible on his knees and look at us over his glasses and say, "What was going on in Rome then?" or "What do you think Indianola looked like at this time?" The way he handled it, the Bible was an exciting story of human life and a part of all history. He had a knack, too, of stopping while we were still eager for more. He never let us get bored. And after he had closed the Bible and settled back in the chair so that we knew he wanted to be left alone, he would say, as he picked up the mystery story some publisher had sent him straight off the press, "Wonderful old boys, those Hebrews. Remarkable. It is no wonder Christ was a Jew."

One time Bun asked him why in the Apostles' Creed we said, "I believe in the Catholic church," when we were Methodists. He made her look "catholic" up in the dictionary. "See that word 'universal'?" he said. "That means the whole world. Everybody is after the same thing. All they want is to be decent so as to be acceptable to God. One tribe tries it one way and another one tries it another way. Some people think foot-washing helps, others burn candles and incense, and many sit in silence and wait. The Good Lord isn't bothered about methods, nor is he too disturbed by our human failings. It's the intentions he cares about."

This kind of talk from a beloved adult when one is still a child has a way of becoming embarrassingly personal. While Bun sat pondering her own sins of recent hours, he said to her, "About the Roman Church, which is what you had in mind when you asked the question, much is to be said of it. If it had not been for the Roman Church there could have been no protesting and so no Protestants. If there had been no Protestants the Roman Church would have allowed itself to get careless and slipshod, which is what happens to any monopoly. Being older, the Roman

Church can teach us a great deal about discipline and organization. Competition is a fine thing, especially when competitors respect one another."

Our first-hand introduction into the ways of the Roman Church came one golden and never-to-be-forgotten summer when we went up to New Ulm, Minnesota, to visit an old school friend of Mother's.

Some families went stodgily to Clear Lake or Okeebojee for the summer. We visited Mother's school friends. Once this landed us in the penitentiary at Walla Walla, where, as guests of the warden's wife, we toured the kitchens and the dining hall. Another time we spent a few stunning weeks with the Blackfoot Indians. There was also an adventure in the Bad Lands when we almost died of thirst. But the visit to the Harry Cains in Mankato was a time of unprecedented joy. Harry Cain had a tile-making factory on the Blue Earth River. He also had a little boy just my age and a girl a little older than Bun, and his idea of entertaining us was to take us sightseeing.

In New Ulm, Minnesota, there is a wondrous statue of a burgomaster in the center of town. Harry Cain took us over to see it, then while Mother and Olive Cain shopped at the German bakery Harry took us to the church, where they had some remarkable and famous Stations of the Cross. Catholic pilgrims came from all over the Middle West to make these Stations. It had not occurred to Mother or to Olive Cain to tell us *not* to make the Stations, so when we got to the broad brick steps that reached up through

the garden of the church, Bun and I and Lawrence
and his sister got down on our knees and made the
Stations of the Cross along with the other pilgrims.
Lawrence did all right. His knickerbockers covered
his knees, but we girls had no such protection.
We crept along over the rough brick, deciding that it
would be irreverent and conspicuous to stand up. By
the time we finished, our knees and legs looked like
raw meat, but so touched were we by this new religious
experience that we did not wince when our startled
mothers washed out the brick dust at the city pump, or
even when they dabbed away infection with raw
alcohol later. Having studied pharmacy, Father had
a disdain for patent antiseptics. It was alcohol or
nothing with him, inside and out.

The New Ulm experience left us with a wholesome
respect for pilgrims, with whom we now felt a kinship.

When we got home, Grandfather inquired about
the scabs on our knees, and we explained a little
archly that we had "made the Stations at New Ulm."
He said he knew about the Stations at New Ulm, that
his friend Father Donovan in Des Moines had described them to him.

This was one of the few times that Grandfather
ever mentioned the priest to us. We all knew that
Grandfather made regular trips to Des Moines. Sometimes he stayed all day, other times only half a day, but
a week never passed without his going up to the capital.
We naturally assumed that he went directly to the
Capitol and there conducted all sorts of important legal

business, and I have no doubt he did just that—first.

But one day, our curiosity aroused, we cornered Grandmother, who told us what Grandfather did with the rest of his time in Des Moines. He spent it with the priest. In fact, even on days when he did not have any business at the Capitol at all, he went to Des Moines anyway to spend the afternoon with the priest.

We could not have been more surprised if Grandmother had told us that Grandfather spent every Thursday afternoon shooting craps in a saloon under the Des Moines viaduct.

Grandfather must have known Father Donovan a very long time, because Grandmother said they were friends when Grandfather was teaching country school and reading law with Uncle Robert Parrott, and that was before the priest had been ordained or Grandfather admitted to the bar.

And it was Father Donovan who taught Grandfather to read Latin and Greek. We were sure that they read poetry together in its original language, because when I was struggling with the *Æneid* in my fourth year of Latin, Grandfather used to recite whole hunks of it at the supper table and then ask me for a quick translation. The parts about Dido, Sibyl and the Shades, and the Funeral Games weren't so bad, but the Mustering of the Tribes left me completely blank. At these times I took a dim view of the priest, but at other times, when Grandfather recited the Hundredth Psalm in Hebrew, just as Father Donovan had taught him, or when he thundered:

> Then outspake brave Horatius,
> The Captain of the Gate;
> "To every man upon this earth
> Death cometh soon or late.
> And how can man die better
> Then facing fearful odds,
> For the ashes of his father,
> And the temples of his Gods,"

I forgave them all the rest.

Our suppers were invariably late on Thursdays, because Grandfather took the six o'clock train down from Des Moines and then walked home from the station, rain or snow, sleet or fair summer weather.

He was always in a good humor on Thursday evenings, and our conversation would be sprinkled with snatches of Irish poetry, a gay limerick or two, or perhaps a learned comment on the social history of England. It was fun to see just what would turn up in Thursday's supper conversation. Grandfather would be in rare form, but there would be no mention of the priest at all. We early learned that Thursday night was the time to ask for an advance on next week's allowance, or, later, to break the news of a Friday night date for the movies.

It was not on a Thursday night at all, however, that we asked Grandmother about the priest.

She always planned a "quick" supper on Thursdays, cold meats and warmed-over vegetables, so we never had much time with her in the kitchen.

It happened at another time, when we were all

at home and when I was so mad at a young female neighbor that I would cheerfully have run her through with a crochet hook and disemboweled her at leisure.

I was standing in the middle of the kitchen, declaiming my side of the story to Grandmother as she ladled the hot navy-bean soup into the white ironstone tureen. I could depend on her loyal agreement that I had been badly treated, even in the face of overwhelming evidence to the contrary.

All of a sudden it was apparent that I had lost my audience. Only Grandfather outranked me in Grandmother's affections, and I turned to find him standing there observing me in twinkling, blue-eyed amusement.

"Bo, I have a friend in Des Moines who has a saying which has been very helpful to me in times like this. Jimmy says, 'Never dignify your enemy with your anger!' "

That night as we washed the dishes I said to Grandmother, "Who is Jimmy?"

Grandmother said, "The priest."

I said, "Why does Grandfather have to be so secret about it all?"

And she said, "He isn't secretive about it. He just likes to keep it to himself. He needs to go to Des Moines and read Greek with the priest just like you need to climb up the old elder tree and build a tree-house. I don't climb up there after you, now do I? And I don't pester your Grandfather about what he does in Des Moines, either."

She carefully assembled the ironstone tureen, platter, lid, and ladle, and bustled off to the dining room with them.

In Iowa you could be what you wanted and worship where, when, and how you wanted. You could believe what you liked and practice your belief. There was, however, one area of rabid intolerance that I learned well as I grew up—that was Iowa's withering rejection of the "Great Agnostic," Robert Green Ingersoll, his theories, practices, writings, etc.

We got the general impression that anyone reading an Ingersoll lecture or, worse yet, attending one given by an Ingersoll disciple, was courting certain death by lightning. But every summer or so the Chautauqua circuit, which at that time welcomed controversial subjects, would slip over one such lecture on the unsuspecting Iowa audience. Then the fat would be in the fire for sure. Grandfather would thunder and Clarence Reynolds would shout and Senator Proudfoot would expostulate, and they would all but run the speaker out of town on a rail and cancel Chautauqua good and plenty for the coming year.

Iowa had then, and has now, Catholics in Dubuque, Mennonites in Amana, Methodists in Indianola, Presbyterians in Cedar Rapids, and Lutherans, Jews, Episcopalians, Congregationalists, and Baptists everywhere.

But atheists and agnostics we didn't have—at least, not for long.

6

THE ARTS AND
THE MULLICANS

Chautauqua wasn't the only cultural influence in our lives, not by a long shot. The "series" was just a concentrated dose we got every summer.

Through the year we had all the artistic diversion we

could comfortably take care of. Simpson College was directly or indirectly responsible for most of this, and not just in the way you might think. It had the usual college lecture series, it is true, but it also had an attitude toward culture which was laudable—even, it would seem, liberal. Grandfather said "they" (he favored the collective pronoun) were not liberal at all. *They* just didn't know any better.

However you looked at it, though, they had let Father and his friend "Mid" go to school tuition free. And with the Conservatory so handy we were bound to be up to here in music, and we were.

Father had been what in those days passed for a pre-med student. When I came along he took a short cut into pharmacy, and from then on continued evermore to be a free-lance. That is, he had too much of the artist in him to stick to anything so static as prescriptions. Then, too, he had studied just enough medicine to be critical of doctors who had earned their diplomas the hard way. That the death rate was no higher among Father's customers than in other parts of the Middle West would seem to indicate either that he knew what he was doing or that Iowans are generally a pretty hardy lot.

It was then the fashion to call druggists "Doc." Father took this to heart. He was never jailed for practicing medicine without a license, but it wasn't his fault. He tried hard enough.

What he really liked to do was sing, and this he could do to the delight of all. His best friend and roommate at Simpson was a large and noble bass-baritone by the name of Arthur Middleton. "Mid" went into music as a career and sang in concert, opera, Chautauqua, the Metropolitan, and Europe.

How Mid got to Simpson is a mystery, but it may be that he was a son of a Methodist preacher. That's how Dad got there. The college took "sons-of" tuition free.

And the town was well paid for its generosity. Dad and Mid tackled oratorios with the same gusto that a Wesleyan end brought to downing a Simpson quarterback. Handel was their favorite, and they executed *Esther, Judas Maccabeus,* and *Samson* with earth-quivering bravura. After they had conquered the trite arias from *Trovatore* and *Rigoletto* they began to treat the audience to bits of Mozart—*Cosi Fan Tutte, Don Giovanni,* and *The Marriage of Figaro.* Meyerbeer they loved, and the Methodist church rocked with selections from *Robert le Diable, Les Huguenots,* and *L'Africaine* on concert nights. Bach's *Passion According to St. Matthew* and *St. John Passion* we got in part and in toto. Mendelssohn's *St. Paul* and *Elijah,* Haydn's *The Seasons,* and Beethoven's *Mount of Olives* were sung to churches with standing room only.

The Messiah was, as is to be expected, an annual event. No matter where we were at Christmas, Father sang the bass solos, and in Iowa people didn't tamper with a composer's score. If Handel wanted it that way, that's the way we got it.

When any member of a family was involved in a

performance the whole family turned out. So year after year we got there early to get a balcony seat. Mother sat in the middle, Bun on one side, me on the other. By the time we got to "Oh, Thou That Tellest," Bun had drooped over, her head resting on Mother's knee. I never lasted much beyond "And Lo, the Angel." But at the first blasts of the organ announcing the "Hallelujah," Mother gave us a whack and we all three jumped to our feet like jacks shot out of a box.

Of all the great oratorios—and when I say all I mean all—the only one I have never heard in its entirety is *The Messiah*. I make the effort year after year, but try as I will somebody always has to wake me up for the "Hallelujah." Father used to say more people got corns from *The Messiah* than from any other piece of music ever written. Corns maybe, but I have to get bruises, too. I am a veteran of *The Messiah* in more ways than one.

Not that Father was limited to a church singer's repertoire—it just happened that that's where the audience was. And when one is sharply limited so far as costume changes, stage sets, and the like are concerned, *The Creation* is easier to put across unassisted than *Aida,* for instance. Although, to Father's credit may it be said, he tried both.

Father had several specialties which he was happy to sing as encores: "The Wind in the Chimney," with words by Bret Harte that sent us children shivering under the bed; "When the Bells in the Belfry Ring Ding Dong," which made us grieve for all men, and "The Flute and Father's Bass" which was happier in mood but strictly a tour de force for low voice.

All this was backed up by the Glee Club and by a diversified instrumental department from the Conservatory, to say nothing of Alice Styre, who could whistle up a storm. She and her husband, Emerson Winter, were on the national concert stage for a while. You don't often hear whistlers like Alice any more.

In the summer, when the college was at peace, the music at church was carried along by a double quartet. Seven of these girls had fine voices. One was Harriet Henderson, who, as Harriet Henders, was later to study abroad and sing at the Metropolitan. Another was Leota Mullican, who had her name changed to Leota Lane by Gus Edwards and is still singing in Los Angeles.

Because it looked better to have an even eight and because the girls were all my friends and because we naturally went to choir practice as well as other places together, they invited me to make up the required number. After about three Sundays, Leota, who was far and away the most diplomatic of the group and a born leader, took me aside and said that she didn't want to hurt my feelings, but since I did not have a "trained" voice and therefore threw the other girls off key, would I mind just holding the hymnal and making my mouth go without actually singing. So I mouthed my way through two, maybe three, summers, and had a wonderful time.

There was a good deal of singing done in Indianola, come to think of it. The boys got out and serenaded the girls in the moonlight. Girls sang three-part harmony on hay rides, sometimes to show off and sometimes to keep busy. We all had ukeleles, which all the girls but I could play. And our repertoire was what you might call classical.

But none of us really thought of music as a profession except Harriet and Leota. Harriet's career turned out to be the usual thing of studying hard, going to Europe, coming home, singing in concerts, getting married, and all that.

Not so with Leota. Now, there was a girl who did it the flashy way.

Leota was the oldest of the Mullican brood. Dr. and Mrs. Mullican lived on our street. Len and Cora B. were not as well mated as most, but better mated than some, for they produced five little girls in biennial succession.

Doc Mullican was the dentist who had his office right opposite Grandfather's on the second floor of the Indianola Bank Building. It may be that he was the best dentist in southern Iowa, but he never really got a chance to prove it because he was a Democrat. Grandfather went to him because he liked Leota's singing, and because Doc was so handy, right across the hall. Grandfather also liked to argue politics, and Doc was the only man in town who could and did take a stand against the Republicans.

What other patients Doc Mullican had came to him because they knew he wouldn't press them for their bills. Being hard up himself and having a wife who thought success was a synonym for wealth, he was sympathetic to the fellow who was up against it. The relay of furtive and indigent Democrats who sneaked up the creaking old stairs to get their teeth fixed was enough to give one the impression that Doc was in the bootlegging business, which everyone knew he wasn't.

Leota looked like Marguerite in Faust—all the time. She had beautiful long blond hair which she braided in a crown around her head, and she started studying at the Conservatory about as soon as she could talk. She made her own dresses from remnants she found on the bargain counter at Charlie Meek's for ten or fifty cents. One particularly dashing costume was made from a piece of striped awning—green, yellow, and orange. Anyone else would have looked like they were sticking out of a rolled-up hammock, but Leota managed to appear chic and slightly Arabic.

Once during the summer when it was fashionable to wear long black cotton stockings with snow white shoes, Leota appeared in a creation that was duplicated years later at a Jacques-somebody-or-other's showing in Paris. The original of this French "original" had had a tightly tucked bodice and a bouffant skirt made out of an old lace curtain bleached white in the sun, draped over a skin-tight sheath off a bolt of Charlie Meek's best black sateen. The charming thing about Leota's being so spectacular was that she was so nice about it.

The next sister was Martha, with whom I share a birthday, a birthplace, an utter lack of musical ability, and a slightly commonplace look that always manages to give us an almost total anonymity in any company numbering more than six.

Martha fooled everyone, though. She grew up and eloped with a Rhodes scholar, the catch of the town, and went to live on college campuses that made ours look like a camp-meeting patch.

The next one was Dorothy. She could sing and she could play the piano. She also had a practical approach to life. Money wasn't everything to Dorothy, it was simply the most important thing.

When we first got the picture show going in Indianola, Dorothy applied for the job of pianist. She did a perfectly tremendous job of it. She was pretty and she marcelled her blond hair in the newest fashion, with puffs and buns and knobs all over her head. She sat at the upright, watching the action and keeping pace with it, while her two little sisters (who got in free), Grandfather, and Scoot sat immediately behind her, cheering her on. Sometimes Scoot would howl and Grandfather would cheer. Then Rosemary would giggle and Priscilla would wiggle in her seat with excitement. But Pearl White would be saved and the Iron Claw done in, and Dorothy would come out even no matter what.

On hot summer nights Grandfather would say, "Bo, how would you like to take in a picture show?" and we'd walk uptown in the soft-scented twilight and go in through the big wide door in the side of the building. The door was only for ventilation. You weren't allowed to use it as an entrance, but Grandfather did. Then he'd go back and pay our admission and we'd settle down in the front row. The piano in this arrangement did not compete with the film, it orchestrated it. The film was silent and flickered, the music was an added attraction.

If Dorothy got there early, Grandfather would lean over and make requests—"The Glow Worm" was a favorite, or "The Beautiful Blue Danube"—and Dorothy would dash these off in whatever tempo would set the mood for the coming feature, usually a fairly rollicking one. Grandfather loved it.

Then would come the slide of the lady wearing the big cartwheel hat, which she seemed to be anchoring with hatpins while a frustrated little man peered out from behind her. This subtle reminder was accompanied by a printed suggestion that "Ladies Will Please Remove Their Hats." This did not directly affect any of us sitting in the front row, all of us being of either the wrong age or the wrong sex to be concerned, but at this point we settled back in our chairs with cheerful expectancy. Dorothy stopped whatever she was playing for Grandfather, and with no more ado began the pastoral accompaniment that introduced even the most blood-curdling holdup or horror tale.

We had just about recovered from the shock of Dorothy's going to Des Moines to get a job in a dairy washing test tubes when a wondrous thing happened. There are probably twenty versions of this story, but I can do justice only to the one I know best:

It seems that Alice MacIntyre, the real good contralto from the girls' double quartet at the First Methodist, had taken a job in a florist shop in Des Moines. Gus Edwards brought his troupe—Lila Lee, George Jessel, etc.—in to town for a week or so. Each night before he went to the theater he stopped at the florist shop to buy himself a boutonnière. Alice was thrilled at her proximity to a celebrity, and she couldn't wait to tell Leota.

Now, Cora B. had been drumming it into the five little Mullicans since birth that they were something special and that they would one day go to the top. So when Leota heard about Gus Edwards, she borrowed the fare from somebody, hopped the Rock Island, and went to Des Moines on the up-early train. She planted herself behind the palms in the florist shop, and when Gus came in to buy his white carnation that night, Leota burst into the "Bell Song."

Leota letting go with the "Bell Song" was something to hear, indeed, and Gus Edwards was the very man to recognize a flair for the dramatic when he heard it. He coaxed Leota out from behind the palms and suggested an audition.

When that magic hour came, Leota showed up with Dorothy. Leota was that way, honest to the core and always eager to share her good luck with the rest of the family.

Well, Gus was slightly disconcerted at seeing two where he had expected one, but not *too* much so, because the other one was Dorothy. No male of any age could look at Dorothy without becoming acutely aware of her. She was titillatingly earthy and refreshingly Iowa all at once. Her skin was peaches and cream. Her figure would, as the boys used to say, "stop a clock." She had the invitingly exciting look of sin you wouldn't be sorry for.

Dorothy's voice was like her piano-playing—lusty, untrained, undisciplined, strident, tireless, effortless, compelling.

Gus Edwards signed the Mullican sisters then and there, and changed their name to Lane because he was superstitious about *l*'s. Lila Lee, his adopted daughter, had brought him nothing but happiness. It was providential that the name Leota began with an *l* already; as for Dorothy, she became Lola.

So, as Leota and Lola Lane, the Mullican girls started out on the road to fame. When they left Indianola for New York it was the sensation of the twenties. Nothing so thrilling had happened in Indianola since Eloise Carpenter married her first millionaire.

Cora B. couldn't go with them. It wasn't that Doc couldn't have got along without her all right. He was sleeping in the office most of the time now anyway, just coming home for dinner, but the two littlest girls were still at home.

Leota took charge of the act from the start. If this older sister ever had any doubts, fears, or reservations, no one ever knew it. Because her heart was pure she had the courage of ten ordinary females, but just to insure their arriving in the big city without incident she fastened her father's Masonic pin to her underwear strap—the theory being that no man worthy of his salt would ravish a girl who was the daughter of a Mason.

In due time the show arrived in Chicago, where by this time a bevy of Indianolaites were working for a living. We turned out in force to cheer the hometown girls. The evening was eventful to me for three reasons. One was that Lola, nee Dorothy, had become so worldly that she talked with a Boston accent, failed to recognize most of us who went backstage, and tipped everybody right and left whether they needed it or not. When I commented on the fact that this profligate distribution of coins of the republic must cut into her earnings more than somewhat, she replied airily with a toss of her head (which was snugly swathed in a turban), "Oh, we don't notice it. We just throw all our silver into the dresser drawer and take our tips from there."

Another thing that made this evening memorable was that Leota was just Leota—serious, worried over Lola's peccadillos, wondering if the show was all right, looking exactly like Marguerite in Faust, and wearing a handsome Parisian frock that looked for all the world as though it had been made out of an awning remnant from the front table at Charlie Meek's.

But the crashing disappointment of the whole evening was Uncle Thad's wife.

Uncle Thad wasn't really an uncle. He was Grandmother's first cousin. In our family we have a lot of staggered generations like that. Somebody three or four years old shows up at the family reunion as uncle to a great oaf in his twenties. Or somebody celebrating his silver wedding anniversary is suddenly confronted with a brother in rubber pants. Grandmother said it was due to the astounding vitality of the Hallam men, but I could never quite believe that the Hallams had a corner on virility.

Anyway, I had heard about Uncle Thad all my life. He was the Beau Brummel, the avant-garde, the bon vivant of the family. He had red hair. He was rich. *And* he had married a chorus girl—one of the original Floradora girls, no less.

Everyone has shattering disillusionments in his life, but that night when I saw our Apollo and his Floradora girl, a lifelong illusion was shattered. Uncle Thad was a thoroughly nice-looking, gray-haired, portly, middle-aged gentleman who wore a common straw hat, smelled very much like our father had, and wore pointed light-brown shoes on his extremely small feet. You wouldn't have looked at him twice on a street car. And as for the chorus girl, she was chuffy and dowdy, less glamorous by far than Belle Banner back home, who had got into trouble in her youth and was working out her penance by keeping twenty-three cats.

So the Lanes toured the country with Gus Edwards and did all right for themselves. Lola went into the movies. Her first picture, I think, was "Speak Easy"— at least, this was the one that electrified Indianola. We really were agog later, though, when she married Lew Ayres.

Dorothy Mullican was a better actress and a prettier one than they ever let Lola Lane be, but as Lola she wiggled, twisted, and shrugged her sultry way through such items as "Girl from Havana," "Murder on a Honeymoon," and "Marked Woman." It is possible that none of these were great movies, but for us they were great fun. After all, there isn't anything much more exciting than seeing somebody you went to school with burst forth on the screen.

So Lola went into the movies, and Leota went to Juilliard. She made her operatic debut in Ravel's *L'heure Espagnol,* in English. Then she sang in concert for a while, and with the St. Louis Opera, and in a plush gambling casino near Pittsburgh.

In the meantime, the two littlest Mullicans had begun to blossom forth. When they said they were going on the stage, folks took them seriously—after all, the stage was a Mullican tradition by now. Their chance came when "Good News," starring Lola Lane, had its premiere in Des Moines. The stage manager, in a flash of intuition, asked Rosemary and Priscilla to appear "in person." This they did to the Queen's taste, and when they went to New York to audition and find numbers for their new act, she went right along with them.

This time there wasn't a thing in the world to keep Corie B. at home. So she pulled up stakes, left dear old 'coon-hunting Len to his drills and dentures, and became—for that time at least—the stage mother to end all stage mothers. From what I could gather, as the Lanes shuttled back and forth through Chicago, Cora B. was three, maybe four, times as effective as a Masonic pin.

One day while Rosemary and Priscilla, at their mother's suggestion, just happened to be at a music publisher's trying out numbers for their act, who should come in but Bobby Crawford. He referred them to Fred Waring, they got an audition, and from then on for a long time they traveled with the Pennsylvanians, with whom they made their first movie, "Varsity Show."

Rosemary was the beautiful one. She had a good bit of what her sister Lola had, only she could sing with it, and her piano work was more disciplined. She made "Hollywood Hotel" with Lola, and married one of the Westmores.

Priscilla was the strange one. She just didn't give a hoop. In our opinion she was the best actress of the lot, but her heart wasn't in it, and when she fell in love she fell out of interest with the theater for good.

As for Cora B., she had the idea that the competitive spirit is the root of all success, so she methodically set about making one sister jealous of another, and the third or fourth envious of the other three. Nothing so stirred Cora B. to her best efforts as to see all five girls happy, relaxed, contented, and at peace with one another.

Grandmother, who had a good word for the devil on occasion and often said that the poor fellow got blamed for a lot of things that weren't really his fault, took up for Cora B. She said it wasn't any picnic living with Doc, and that with five little girls to sew for no wonder she was nervous. Grandmother said that the four little Mullicans would never have gotten anywhere at all without their mother. But to some of us it seemed possible that they would have gone a lot further, once they had got started, if their mother hadn't hovered over them like a brood hen with a flock of guineas. Of course, every mother is ambitious for her children in one way or another— Cora B. just stuck to it harder than most. And it must be admitted that she had better material to work with than some.

The culmination of the Lane sisters' career was, so far as their Indianola fans were concerned, the picture "Four Daughters." It was based on fact, and Lola, Priscilla, and Rosemary were in it. Leota was tested, but unfortunately replaced. It's too bad that all the Mullicans weren't signed up for that picture—no matter how much Claude Rains resembled Doc, he wasn't Doc; only Leota could sing like Leota; and no one could play Cora B. but Cora B. herself. Also, we couldn't help feeling that motion picture audiences across the country were cheated a little by being confronted with a sugary-sweet household instead of the true-to-life Mullican formula of earthy gusto, free-swinging individualism, and exquisite optimism.

As for Doc and what he thought about all this, he never said.

He moved back into the old brown house on West Ashland Avenue after Cora B. left with the rest of the girls. He set up his office in the front room where the piano had been, and filled teeth and looked out the window and talked about how the girls had given him the house free and clear. He never talked about the college's ever having owned the house, but after the back rent was paid and the deed was in his desk drawer he delighted in telling anyone who would stand still and listen how good his girls were to him.

It may have been Henry Wallace who got Doc appointed postmaster in Indianola, since they had gone 'coon hunting together, but whoever stands to get the credit for it, the appointment was undoubtedly one of the most popular under a Roosevelt administration.

The Republicans thought that as long as they were beat and had to have a Democrat it was a good thing to have a fellow like Doc, whom you could trust.

The Democrats, who showed up in the light for the

first time as a careworn minority, felt it was no more than Doc deserved, and picture-crazy folks liked seeing the father of four movie stars come forward to help out with parcels and stamps.

There were some who declared it was good enough for Cora B., after running off and leaving Len that way, that she should find herself way off in California in a flat-top ranch house while Len was right here in Indianola—cozy as a moth in a minister's pants pocket —with a position of importance and a good income.

In addition to the "spectacular" aspects of the arts, Indianola had its quieter moments of self-expression. Mother and Aunt Margaret were whizzes at the charming craft of china painting, which was all the rage then.

It began with Tiffany's bringing over from England sometime about 1870 a man whose name was Bennett and whose craft was china painting. From this little acorn, a forest of hand-painted everything grew. The "blanks" were white china, usually of good lines and almost always imported. Each china painter had a box of paints, a glass plate on which to mix them, oils, turpentine, silk paint-rags, and stencils, the last-mentioned item depending upon whether or not one painted free-hand. The wild rose in delicate shades of pink was one of Mother's favorites. Aunt Margaret, who had less talent at this than Mother, stuck with forget-me-nots. We had hat-pin holders, powder jars, dresser trays, pepper and salt shakers, cups and saucers, bread-and-butter plates, and pickle dishes in various patterns of forget-me-nots and wild roses.

Mother's conventional designs won prizes. Purple grapes with green leaves and a gold border made a stunning decoration for a mayonnaise bowl. The geometric patterns done in enamel on cups and bread-and-butter plates were the pride of our lives. How anyone could be as clever as Mother we couldn't see, but Grandfather wasn't impressed. He said china painting was ruining him, and that it was an underhand promotion scheme of the china importers to sell more and more sets of china. Not only were the "blanks" expensive, and these showed up frequently enough on Allie Miller's bill, but each piece of china had to be fired in a kiln maintained for this purpose and there was, naturally, a kiln fee—in addition to all of which there were lessons to be paid for. Grandfather said it would have been cheaper to send all three of them, meaning Grandmother, Mother, and Aunt Margaret, up to Des Moines and let them run loose in Brinsmaid's china store.

Aunt Dot said he ought to be proud that Mother was studying with a woman who had studied with Etta Budd, who had studied with Rachael Taylor, who had been a pupil of the great Bennett himself. Aunt Dot was very proud of having been a pupil of Miss Etta Budd, and it was in Miss Budd's class that she had worked at the easel right next to George Washington Carver. She never called him anything but George-

Washington-Carver, either, and she said it had been a privilege to sit next to him in art class, not because he was a great painter, which he wasn't, or because he was famous, but because he was a great artist at the skill of living.

One day when I was complaining about what a tank town Indianola was and how nobody had ever heard of Simpson College, Aunt Dot said, "It was good enough for George-Washington-Carver, and it's good enough for you. It was right there in Miss Etta Budd's painting class that George-Washington-Carver said to me in the spring of ninety-one, 'Miss Hamilton, I have just made an exciting discovery. I am a human being.'

"Pray God you learn as much !".

7

SOCIAL SECURITY

The only people who ever retired in the days before
Social Security were Methodist ministers and "dirt"
farmers.

The ministers retired, so Grandfather said, so that

they could sit on the front porch of the Old Men's Home and belabor each other with their sermons. In a manner of speaking, Grandfather was allergic to Methodist ministers, excepting his opposite number, my Grandpa Smith, who almost literally died in harness.

William Henry Harrison Smith had no business being a minister in the first place, according to my Grandfather Brown. Smith was a Virginia gentleman who delighted in his life and lived it well. Through an irresponsible quirk of fate he got up Philadelphia way before The War and married a Miss Rebecca Pendergast who lived to be ninety-four years old.

Rebecca, who was the size and weight of an overgrown child, was an orphan, and she had all the assertive ways that a resourceful child tends to develop when left to fend for herself. She must have realized early the advantages of being "poor little motherless Becky." At any rate, William Henry Harrison, who was a most unlikely Methodist, a leisurely preacher, and a peace-loving man, got sent off to fight for the Union with a Northern regiment.

The fact that his father and two of his brothers were "with Virginia" may have slackened his fervor, or it may have been the fact that Rebecca was comfortably a thousand miles away, but as it turned out William Henry Harrison spent most of The War in Libby prison. We had several remarkable and singular trophies to show for it. One was the Lord's Prayer carved in wood and embellished with a golden eagle. This hung in the dining room. Then there was a pair of salad spoons, and a fork with roses on the handle. Mother gave these to Grandmother, who used them only for Alonaidni. And then there was a fat walnut robin with a hole in his belly designed to hold one soft-shelled pecan. When you twisted his tail, the nut cracked. Since the only nuts known to Iowa are so hard they can only be cracked with a flat-iron and hammer, we kept the Libby prison robin on the library table for show.

Grandpa Smith and Rebecca had six children, each conceived, born, and reared in a different town. For instance, Uncle Ed could have been conceived in Spencer, born in Redoak, and raised in Perry. Grandpa Smith just never got the same "call" twice. He was on the go. While nobody mentioned it, the general feeling was that this transient state of Reverend Smith had something to do with horse-racing.

Coming from Virginia as he did, Grandpa liked horses, and this was one thing Rebecca never could quite iron out of him. So it was his custom to deliver a hellfire sermon as hot as the real thing, stop off for chicken and dumplings at one of the stewards' homes, and then, on his way back to town, ride the long way around to the nearest county fair or horse-racing event.

Sulkies were his favorite, but he wasn't fussy. Any kind of horse race would do. Grandpa himself was the best rider in those parts, and always kept a spanking team of his own—*too* spanking to suit his congrega-

tion. It was unseemly, people thought, for the preacher
to come out of his church, leap into the saddle, and rein
up his mount in a flurry of prancing and whinnying and
kicking of forefeet before taking off down the road at
a breeze-splitting gallop, his white beard waving and
the tails of his black coat flapping behind him.

Grandfather said *there* was a man who would not
be caught dead going to the Methodist Home for
Retired Preachers. He wasn't.

This refuge of the weary was the source of many
a joke between Grandfather and his best friend, Hiram Sedgwick.

Professor Sedgwick was probably the handiest kind
of friend a lawyer could have. No matter what else
came along in the world of litigation, Grandfather
always had Sedgwick to defend, not only in court
against the Masons of Davenport and Sedgwick's
own kith, kin, wife, and partners—to name but a few
—but at board meetings and by mail, phone, and tele-
graph. Between crises, Grandfather still had Sedgwick to advise, admonish, and cuss out. No wonder
Grandfather adored Sedgwick to the bitter end. He
was practically indispensable.

It could be that Sedgwick had at one time taught
mathematics et cetera at Simpson College, and picked
up "The Professor" title that way. But this, like everything else about Sedgwick, present and past, was veiled
by a mist of uncertainty. There was nothing obscure
about his future, though. According to Grandmother he

would surely wind up behind bars sooner or later, because not even Grandfather could stop the inexorable processes of justice.

Sedgwick invented two gadgets for trains. One was a chronograph which, when attached to a locomotive, would record every detail: speed, whistle-blowing, braking, irregularities in the track, cows run over— in fact, just about everything. The great question, and it is still open, was whether Sedgwick ever really intended to manufacture the chronograph. That he said he did was no guarantee. He took out the patent May 2, 1899, and with this in hand started selling large blocks of stock in the American Chronograph Company. Grandfather was the attorney for the company. Grandmother wouldn't let Grandfather invest in anything Sedgwick had anything to do with, so his pay for legal services was to be in stock.

In the years that followed, the chronograph went through some mighty fancy doings. These involved several eastern railroads, a Mrs. Hettie Richards, and a Presbyterian preacher from Pittsburgh.

Mrs. Sedgwick felt she had been deserted and left with two children to starve in Des Moines. This problem she took up with Grandfather. "Prof" was living at Hettie's house in Chicago, calling her the secretary of the company and taking her along on his trips to Brooklyn in case the finance committee should need a transcript in the middle of the night. This looked a little irregular even to Grandfather, who advised his friend to "return home on separate trains, because gossip in Des Moines is bad and in Chicago it is even worse."

The chronograph was tried out, happily on a test basis, by a railroad in New England. Satisfied with the first performance, the officers of the railroad company proposed becoming officers of the American Chronograph Company, guaranteeing sufficient orders from their railroad and others in which they were substantial shareholders to get the new business "off the ground."

Although the correspondence involved would pretty well prove that this idea was as much Sedgwick's as was the invention itself, Grandfather was indignant at the plan. In fact, he used it as the basis of an article on the immorality of trusts, which he wrote for the *Legal Journal.*

Sedgwick, who could talk out of both sides of his mouth about as well as anybody, assured Grandfather that he was mistaken in his harsh judgment of the plan. But the wife of a Presbyterian minister in Allegheny City, across the river from Pittsburgh, also held the harsher view, and, since it was her money that was invested, convinced her husband to urge Grandfather to take a trip to New York and look into the matter.

Two notable things happened on this trip. While he was standing on the corner of Madison and State in Chicago, between trains, a little boy came up to him and said something. Grandfather happened to be looking at his watch just then, and being deaf besides did not hear the boy. So he asked him to repeat what he had said. After about three rounds of this, Grandfather said, "Oh, so you want to know the time? It is a quarter to seven." .

"So!" replied the child in a bellow to be heard by the lions in Lincoln Park. "When it gets to be seven o'clock you can kiss my behind!"

And in New York, during one of the tense meetings on the organization and refinancing of the chronograph operation, Grandfather walked to a window and looked out on Wall Street. He was quickly joined by one of the railroad's attorneys. "Quite a city isn't it, Mr. Brown?" the fellow said.

Grandfather nodded.

The New York lawyer waved his arm with a gesture of abundance, "I've been out West a time or two myself. Once to Buffalo and twice as far as Pittsburgh. Nice country you have out there."

Grandfather went back to the meeting and won the debate that day. He said anybody *that* stupid couldn't know much law either. Maybe he didn't, but nobody ever made any money out of the chronograph but Hiram Sedgwick.

His train-stopper might have had a chance if Grandfather could have proved Hiram hadn't stolen it from George Westinghouse or vice versa. By the time this case came to trial Sedgwick had gotten a national reputation for duplicity, and Grandfather had grown so impatient of the machinations of big business that much of the steam had gone out of the grievance.

Nevertheless, Grandfather liked to have Sedgwick around.

Grandmother thought all this talk about fortunes to be made in train-stoppers and chronographs was so much tomfoolishness, and said so. Besides, she didn't like Sedgwick's flirtatious ways. He was what is now known, and doubtless was then known, as a "pincher." But Grandfather loved having the Professor around, and they would sit in the park or up in the square or on our front porch or out under the willow tree by the hour or by the day talking about literature or people or poetry or music. Sometimes they would read out loud to each other, but this was rarely necessary since both of them could quote by the chapter.

Early one morning they were sitting out on the porch right under my bedroom window. I heard Grandmother go downstairs about seven o'clock, tipping lightly on the stairs. She never left the second floor without being fully dressed, her hair combed, her face powdered lightly, her housedress crackling with starch, and her ankles trim and neat above her carefully polished oxfords.

This morning she walked out onto the front porch and said, "Well, good morning. What would you two like for breakfast this morning?"

Grandfather, knowing that Sedgwick was a prodigious eater and that he probably hadn't eaten for a day or so, having just that morning come down to

Indianola on the early train, said, "How about a gentleman's breakfast?"

Grandmother said, "And what do you consider a gentleman's breakfast?"

Grandfather said, "Oh, ham or steak and eggs, fried mush, hot biscuits, fried potatoes, strawberry preserves, and coffee."

"Gentleman's breakfast?" Grandmother said, and she walked down to the front walk and looked up the street and down, shading her eyes from the early morning sun. When she came back she said, "Are you expecting somebody, Papa?"

Sedgwick must have been a member of the Bible Club, too. He was an authority on the Bible, and could preach sermons if anybody would let him. The Bible Club was the gayest club Grandmother belonged to, and she was a joiner if there ever was one. The Bible Club was co-educational, and was not confined either to the study of the Bible or to members who could show their Methodist baptismal card. It was the one social thing Grandfather would do.

Benny and Mona Clayton were members, and Sig and Martha Burberry and the Andersons and the Pearlies, and the meetings were dinner meetings. Sam White and his current wife came to look after things and there was much excitement all over the house for days before a Bible Club meeting. Curtains were washed and books dusted and things carted up to the attic by the armload. The beds were covered with the best and newest quilts and the rag rugs were washed and fluffed, and Sam went over the floors with a hand polisher. Mother said the nicest thing about having company was that the house was so clean and neat for the family afterward.

Before Bible Club even the privy had to be whitewashed. We never did use it much except as a convenience since we had the inside one, but Grandmother said Benny Clayton couldn't go upstairs with his bad foot and Grandfather said it was handier for the men. So Grandmother would tell Sam to be sure to knock down the wasps.

We had our specialites for the Bible Club, and these the members learned to depend on. There was corn soup to start with, followed by chicken pie with little new potatoes, pearl onions, and the little unborn egg yellows that turned up inside Auntie Flummer's stewers.

Grandmother was famous for her macaroni and cheese and perfection salad. Vegetables we had in season or canned. Fresh vegetables were boiled and served with butter, but canned vegetables needed fixing. Aunt Margaret had a recipe for "sweet and sour" wax beans that was a hit. Tomatoes came to the table baked with peppers and rice for parties or company. Carrots and parsnips were browned in butter, but were rarely presented for company fare since everybody had carrots and parsnips in the root-cellar.

In the spring we had strawberry shortcake for dessert, and this was expected of us since Grandmother's recipe for the delicacy was the best in town. If strawberries were gone, cherry cobbler might do. There was a season for fresh raspberry sherbet with imperial cookies. And one for fresh peach pie, and, in their time, mince tarts with "vanilla."

Mother had a specialty called "ground-cherry preserve." Only Father, in all the world, apparently, knew how to raise ground cherries, which grew on a little bush about the size of a hot-pepper plant. The seed pod was like a hickory nut, the same color and size, and inside this pod was a small berry something like a gooseberry. When the pod turned beige in color Mother harvested these berries, mixed them with fresh peaches, and made ground-cherry preserve. Mother also did a "spice" grape to the queen's taste. Usually Grandmother scorned these vagaries, concentrating on the straight-away open kettle pear or plum, but when Bible Club met she was always glad to have Mother offer a jar of her ground-cherry preserve.

Maybe they had a business meeting after the dinner and maybe they had a planned program, but it seemed to me that every time I walked through the library or across the porch or through the pantry, the periphery of the meeting, I could hear Grandfather expounding his theories on the personality of George Westinghouse or the genius of Ambrose Bierce or the dramatic reaches of the *Tales of Hoffman* or the pusillanimous curricula of modern education. It didn't sound very biblical to me—just Grandfather taking the floor and sounding off to a bigger-than-usual audience.

When Grandmother was around Grandfather, she let him take over and do the talking, and he did. She went about her work, cooking, or serving the plates, or sewing quilt scraps, with only an occasional "Yes, Papa," but you knew she wasn't half paying attention.

With the Shakespeare Club it was something else again. There she had her say.

The Shakespeare Club was a cultural organization —most exclusive—of ladies who knew *Twelfth Night* from Midsummer same and were proud of it. They had very fancy programs called "Year Books" printed up at the *Herald* office, on the front page of which was a fine, bold engraving of Mr. Shakespeare. We had a large marble bust of the bard on the piano in the sitting room. No doubt other members revered his memory in a similarly suitable way. Grandmother had books on Stratford-on-Avon and early theater and I don't know what-all, which belonged especially to her and were kept in a three-section book case with folding glass fronts. Grandfather's books were open to the air, dust, mice, and an occasional swallow, but not Grandmother's. Hers were carefully kept under glass, and so was Shakespeare.

When the Shakespeare Club met at the house, we girls all had to help. This was mostly a matter of getting out the good china, the good silver, and appropriate table decorations, since the Shakespeare Club kept the menu down to a small snack—apple or cherry turnovers, lemon ice or peach ice cream, fruit cake and angel food, date tarts, macaroons, chocolate dainties, penuchi, snowballs, peanut clusters, coffee, tea, and fruit punch.

Then there was the D.A.R., which started and ended with Grandmother. She had been a member of the D.A.R., Des Moines chapter. Finally she got to be several kinds of chairwoman, but it seemed pretty certain she would never make Regent. This sorry plight prevailed in spite of the fact that her brother Willie was a leading light in the S.A.R. chapter in the capital.

Uncle Willie took being an S.A.R. seriously. It was about the most serious thing in his whole life.

He and Grandmother and Aunt Dot were all Hamiltons; and when Uncle Willie got to nosing back in his family line he found a connection with Alexander Hamilton. Uncle Willie was impetuous. He was given to jumping at conclusions, and in those days he could afford it.

He had an iron foundry which was doing pretty well on the banks of the Des Moines River. After a little while the Des Moines Steel Company came along and knocked Uncle Willie's iron foundry into a trivet, and the Des Moines Hamiltons fell upon lean days. This went hard with them. Nina, the eldest, had been real busy living in the rarefied atmosphere of society and the two boys had done their share to keep the family insolvent. They had had a car when automobiles were not to be got into lightly, and they lived in the best part of town in a house we thought dark and ugly because it had so little lawn.

It was during those halcyon days that Uncle Willie gave the state of Iowa his gun collection, which is still, so far as I know, exhibited in one of the corners of the rotunda at the state Capitol. And it was about then that Uncle Willie discovered Alexander Hamilton. Being such a hell-for-leather Son of the American Revolution he must have known better, but the joys of ancestry have corrupted better men than Uncle Willie. That he was descended from Alexander of Grange, the grandfather of Alexander the Federalist, seemed certain enough. So he went out and got a costume to make himself look like the man whose life Burr's bullet put to a sudden and dramatic end. The resemblance was striking, it was true, if Trumbull's portrait could be trusted, and so Uncle Willie sat himself down in a chair in a pose he considered proper and had his picture taken.

The results were so heartening that Uncle Willie lost his head completely and sent his picture broadcast among the family.

Grandmother thought it was real good of Willie.

Grandfather laughed until he cried. He could hardly wait until Uncle Willie drove down on Sunday in the Maxwell for chicken and noodles. "Well, Willie," Grandfather said, "we got your picture. It's the best photograph of a bastard we've had around here in a long time."

It was Uncle Willie who had the last laugh, though.

Just about the time he was ready to admit that the only hope left was for Belle to take in roomers, the state decided to beautify its Capitol grounds, and there stood Uncle Willie's foundry right in the path of beauty and improvement.

The forge was cold and the anvil rusty, but by the time Uncle Willie got through with the condemnation appraisers that property on the river bank was so valuable it ranked next to equal footage on Times Square.

So the Des Moines Hamiltons sold out and went West. No covered wagons for them. It was Santa Fe all the way. And when they got there Uncle Willie invested in a string of duplex apartments of the renting kind. The Des Moines Hamiltons never had to worry again.

Well, Grandmother decided she might get some kind of office out of it in the Abigail Adams chapter, especially since Willie had given the state his gun collection and sold them the river bank property, but when it became clear that she would never make Regent she pulled out to organize a chapter in Indianola. Martha Devotion, which was what its name was, would have caught on better if there hadn't been so many other clubs around. In those days, before ready-mix cupcakes, frozen melon balls, and TV dinners, there was just so much any one woman could do away from home in a week. So Grandmother was Organizing-regent, but hard put to it to keep Martha Devotion chapter up to charter quota. The girls passed the regency around among themselves for a while, and Grandmother got to represent her chapter in state meetings and in Washington, D.C., a time or two, but when the novelty of this began to wear off and when she could no longer be as active as she once was, Martha Devotion began to peter out.

In the meantime, Grandmother had got herself several bars to hang below her pin. Each of these represented a "line" that went back to the Revolution. You only had to prove your connection with one line in order to belong to the Daughters of the American Revolution. Grandmother got in on the Hamilton line, then proved up the Flemings, the Hallams, the Sillicks, and the Lyons, so she had a bar to prove that each one of these colonial farmers was both fecund and patriotic. Mother, who was always in a kind of contest with Grandmother, decided she would get herself some bars, too, and ended up with sixteen fastened below her D.A.R. pin. It was a sight to see. It looked like she had just won all the markmanship matches at a national guard encampment.

P.E.O. was a sorority and secret order to which town girls were eligible. In order to be a member of one of the Greek sororities associated with the college you had to be a student there, and one in good standing. Aunt Margaret was always a student of sorts at the college and elsewhere, but never one in good standing. It wasn't that Aunt Margaret was dumb. She just wasn't interested. P.E.O., it seems, was a club for ladies who either couldn't or didn't want to

go to college. Its insignia was a five-pointed star with
"P.E.O." on it, and its flower was a daisy. Since both
Aunt Margaret and Grandmother were members, and
since all this was in the heyday of china painting, we
existed at meals in a sargasso sea of daisies, five-
pointed stars, and P.E.O. colors, yellow and white.
Not one of the rest of us knew what it meant, but
P.E.O. was with us as constantly as white bread and
butter. We have a picture somewhere of a meeting of
this club. All the girls are arranged in tiers on our
front steps. Some of them are wearing band suits and
bandmasters' caps with gold braid and frogs. Aunt
Margaret and Calla McNeil even have false mus-
taches. I don't suppose the latter was strictly necessary
to become a member but it made us wonder.

Then there was the Masonic Lodge.

Grandfather was a red-hot Mason, and he believed
in Masonry so firmly that he offered to pay the way
for his two sons-in-law through the degrees. Uncle
George didn't get very far. He was too nervous, but
my father was a free-loader by birth, instinct, and
choice. He would go anywhere, eat anything, do anything anyone suggested if there was no expense involved. Not that Father was a tightwad—far from
it. He was the most generous of human beings. He
just figured that if the other fellow thought enough of
him or of the project to finance it and invite him to
participate, the least he could do to show his appreciation was to accept and cooperate.

On this theory Father went to the top in Masonry.

He had a hat with a beautiful white plume and a sword in a scabbard, and no one cut a handsomer figure than our father at funerals. If Father's good nature could have been confined to Masonry it would have been all right. Unfortunately for us, he was accommodating in other ways. As handsome as a male can be and still be male-looking, Father had regular, aristocratic features. He also had thick black eyebrows and long eye-winkers, and skin so pink and white you had to look twice to be sure he wasn't made up for the theater or something. His eyes were blue, and they sparkled with an agreeable detachment, as though he was laughing at the world. His lips, which were red and full, carried a secret smile that made dimples at the corners of his mouth. He was not really flirtatious. He just looked that way. And looking the way he did, it was easy to understand his almost electric effect on women. Coupled with gay good looks and the voice of an angel, his generous, accommodating nature made it almost impossible for him to find time for anything but pleasure. There were scarcely days or hours enough to go round. There was nothing of your leering, pawing, snorting, lecherous old roué about Father. He was, on the contrary, always a little apologetic that life had seen fit to channel his talents into the path of the primrose. Nor did he blame any second, third, fourth, or fifth party for his defections. At the moments of his not-infrequent indictments he invariably took full responsibility. You don't often run across a man as generously gallant as my father.

And, of course, there was the Eastern Star. Grandfather saw to it that Grandmother, Mother, and Aunt
Margaret all joined, the latter as soon as they were
old enough to wear long white dresses. This made for
one more secret society in our household. People don't
seem to be the secret-keepers they once were. We had
fraternity secrets (father was an A.T.O.), sorority
secrets (Mother and our cousin Fairie Mae were Tri
Delta), society secrets (Aunt Margaret and Grandmother being P.E.O.), and Grandfather carried all the
secrets of Masonry and his profession in his bosom.
Everyone was respectfully allowed to keep his own secrets (except Father, but then his sometimes got a little
out of hand). We children had secrets, too—not that
they amounted to much, but to us they were nearly
sacred.

Dorothy Hopper and I were in the pantry one day,
hunting for the fruit cake Grandmother had stashed
away against Thanksgiving and the holiday influx of
the Des Moines Hamiltons, when we heard whispering
and giggling in the dining room. So we listened.

It seems that the night before at the Eastern Star
initiation, Mother had been the door-keeper or ser-
geant-at-arms or whatever. The Worthy Matron for
that term was a lady of some political charm and
personal means, but she was a little lean on education.
When the door-keeper, who was Mother (and I must
say she had looked pretty elegant getting off to lodge,
her long white hand-drawn linen dress making an in-
congruous blob of white in the autumn twilight) an-

nounced the candidate, she said some words to the effect that the candidate waited without. This particular girl (according to Mother and Aunt Margaret) was stuck-up, a snob with a head too big for her bonnet. Imagine Mother's hilarious delight when the Worthy Matron called out loud and clear, "Omit her!", and then, after a hasty bit of prompting from the next chair, amended her decision by bellowing, "Admit her!"

We didn't think this was very funny, not nearly so side-splitting as Aunt Margaret and Mother, who laughed until tears came to their eyes. But we were impressed with the fact that we were now bearers of secrets of the inner circle. We felt as though we had already made a start toward the chairs—had gotten a "leg up," as it were. (And I did make Pi Phi in my college days later on.)

The nearest thing to a service club in Indianola was Alonaidni, which is, of course, Indianola spelled backwards. It was a woman's club dedicated to good works.

This meant seeing to it that the city kept the grass mowed in Buxton Park and that the benches were kept painted on the courthouse lawn. Generally, Alonaidni kept its eye on things, and its way of working was not to make a public issue of its good intentions by storming the courthouse or bedeviling the mayor. The ladies met once a month. They took their sewing and ate quantities of peach fluff in meringue shells and drank quarts of hot or iced tea, according to the season. When some matter of civic importance came before the club, the course of action was determined after discussion and resolution passed. There the matter rested officially, but that night at dinner all the husbands of Alonaidni got a report of the meeting with their cold supper. Each woman in her own way put the bee on her husband to accomplish said good work.

The next day, at the courthouse or over the counter or on the corner, Mr. Pearlie and Judge Proudfoot compared notes. Before the next meeting of Alonaidni the project was on the rails or the mission had been accomplished, and the members could go on to the next civic improvement. These civic improvements were not always permanent. For example, there was the rule against spitting tobacco juice on the platform of the Rock Island station. The evidence of public opinion was written on the record and on the station master's slate board: "The Alonaidni requests no Spitting Tobacco. This Means YOU!" And the nuisance might be said to have been diminished appreciably, at least until the sign became a familiar part of the décor, which didn't take long.

With such a ladies' auxiliary there was no need for a chamber of commerce, Rotary club, or civic service club. Sooner or later in a given week every man of any importance was sure to run into some other man of equal importance "on the square" and thus Alonaidni's concept of civic virtue usually became public opinion. Since every man who could, which was the majority of home owners, went home for his dinner, which was

served in the middle of the day, there was small opportunity for "luncheon" clubs or meetings. Supper meetings were confined to church activities. These might be
Oyster suppers or Box suppers or Family suppers or
Missionary suppers, but their purpose was limited to
some phase of church support.

Grandfather and his friends would have looked
upon the "committee" system as being an infringement
of the rights of the individual, or at best an indictment
of his ability to get things done as a householder.

The privilege of being a householder entailed certain
responsibilities. There were such obvious duties as
keeping one's house painted, lawn trimmed, and sidewalk swept clean of leaves and shoveled free of snow.
But there were other requisites to being a member of
a community. One was to see that one's children be-
haved their bratty little selves.

Our eyes bugged out as our parents regaled us with
stories of the whippings they had got as children. We
never were larruped in the old sense of having one's
pants pulled down in the woodshed and being lashed
with a leather belt. But we got spanked. Once I got
it so hard I had to sit on one cheek for two days. It
happened late in my childhood, when I was so big
Mother had to stretch me out on my stomach on the
old black leather couch. She was mad as hops, and she
whacked me as hard as she could with the sole of her
slipper, holding it firmly by the French heel. I remember to this day precisely why she whacked me. I
knew then, too, and even as I yelled and sobbed and

protested, I knew she was right. I never did it again. If I had, I probably would have ended up in Omig Row, and if you don't know where Omig Row is, all you need to know about it is that it is no place to end up in—or start out in, either.

We had, broad and long, early and late, generally and specifically, a wholesome respect for law, order, and the head of the house.

If there was an extra piece of pie left from dinner, Grandfather would have it for supper. If there was one piece of white meat on a platter among a welter of wings, backs, and second joints, Grandfather got the piece of breast without the shadow of a question.

We had a curfew, and someway or other we managed to abide by it. We did not run wild even as teenagers. We reported in at specified times. We asked permission to leave the premises. We shut up in front of our elders, and we tried to make ourselves scarce at chore times. The only clear-cut privilege of being a teen-ager was that it gave you a turn at washing the dishes. Helping with the dishes was something you did three times a day from birth—or so it seemed. Drying became your job the day you were coordinated enough to hold a dish towel, and you were elevated to "putting away" as soon as your legs were long enough to bring you within reach of the cup hooks. But *washing* the dishes was the last step—the sign that you had matured. At about this time you also became eligible for Epworth League, which you could attend at seven

o'clock Sunday night. The boys could walk home behind you at eight. You had about as much chance to
create a teen-age problem as a colt tied to a gatepost.
You could kick up your heels, but you couldn't get very
far.

There was a kind of warm security in the knowledge
that you wouldn't get away with any nonsense, even
when you tried, because it was the express duty of the
head of the household to keep you in line. He knew it.
You knew it. The town held him accountable.

The head of the household was responsible for the
family bills and he paid them. He sometimes raised
Cain about them. But he paid them. If he couldn't pay
them right that minute he made arrangements.

We early learned that the Lord Himself was on the
side of parents. If we *did* sneak off for a picnic in
Pheiffer's Woods when we should have been picking
beans for Auntie Marsh, the Lord invariably pushed
us into the creek so that we would arrive home
dripping, shamefacedly acknowledging our duplicity.
Or if we went out to the fairgrounds to play follow-
the-leader over the empty cow-barn stalls when we
should have been cleaning the attic, the Lord knocked
us out of an empty mow and we broke an arm. You
can take just so much of this kind of thing. After a
while you decide it is all-around easier to ride tether.
Any other way the odds are stacked against you.

Once the Lord went so far as to let an old Lincoln
Standard Biplane come unglued over the state fair-

grounds just to prove that He was on Grandfather's side. The fact that the pilot and I walked away from a crash landing in a cornfield behind the cow-barns would have seemed an encouraging sign, had not a photographer from the Des Moines *Register* been right on hand with a loaded camera. His handiwork appeared the next day over the caption, "Simpson College Co-ed Survives Air Crash over State Fairground." It seemed to me then that this was making a pretty big thing out of skipping one chemistry lab.

Well, that's how it was. So many families, so many kingdoms, and no king ever thought for a minute of abdicating unless he had put his sweat into farm land, in which case he just sold out and moved to Long Beach, California, to get a good rest. The doctors, the lawyers, the merchants, even the bankers kept on working. They liked to. They didn't want to step down from their place in the community. The older a man got the more his seniority built up. Grandfather said there were men he knew around town who hadn't sense enough to come in out of the rain, but, because they were old, spoke with the authority of Joshua and the finality of St. Paul. Grandfather was, however, a tough critic to please.

He never thought of retiring. When he got to be past eighty he slowed down a little. He only walked back and forth to the square twice a day instead of three or four times, and he took to sleeping late in the mornings, not arriving at his office much before seven-thirty. We noticed that he would read for a half-hour or so after dinner before picking up his hat and starting back uptown for the afternoon.

There was, of course, an economic factor as well as a prideful interest in the profession or the town that determined a man's continued concern. Incomes were not great even for bankers, and though living was not high, certain obligations always had to be met. Any man of substance had his own "charges," which he accumulated through his lifetime. There were certain families that Dr. Baker birthed, tended, and looked after, and everyone knew these were "Doc Baker's cases." Not completely indigent, they still could not pay doctor bills, so they didn't. Doc Mullican carried the matter to an extreme, filling, all for free, the teeth of those unstable individuals who espoused the Democratic party or who were too poor to assert themselves Republican.

Charlie Meek kept oilcloth and calico remnants just for his non-paying customers. And many the sack of dried beans or onions or dried apples or corn meal that was dropped off the Anderson and Pearlie truck at homes where Mrs. Pearlie had seen children looking poorly.

People repaid these courtesies in the best way they could. Dr. Baker or George Pearlie might look out his back window some morning to find a whole cord of stove-wood stacked neatly against the woodshed. Or Mrs. Orr might find a stack of carefully hemmed, initialed tea towels on top of a crock of country butter when she went out to the pump. The best tea towels in the world are made from flour sacks washed in lye soap, bleached in the sun, and hemmed all around with featherstitching.

Chickens were a favorite tender for Grandfather, also wild plums, wild grapes, hickory nuts, and country sausage, but he also received various baked goods like Auntie Marsh's bread and Mrs. Condit's cakes. Mrs. Condit was a widow who knew that Grandfather loved hickory nuts. To show her appreciation for his legal advice and guidance, Mrs. Condit laboriously picked and cracked piles of hickory nuts and baked fluffy cupcakes that he adored—and we did, too. Grandmother put the Condit cakes high up in the pantry where we couldn't reach them, to save them for Grandfather's supper. If we did find them, slip one out and rearrange the plate, we always got the only one that had a shell in it. After chipping two "second teeth" even the greedy would be inclined to let Grandfather have his cupcakes. It was a never-ending mystery to us why there were never any shells in the Condit cakes *he* ate.

It now seems hard to believe that this back-door barter of service and bounty could have been carried on without any embarrassment or self-conscious demur, but it was. Only once in our experience did the system "backfire," and it couldn't have happened at a worse time.

It was the night before Thanksgiving.

Grandfather had called Grandmother early in the day to say someone had left a heavy package that felt like a turkey in the office when he had gone to the post office. Grandmother said, "Fine. Never mind going past Emil's then. Just bring it on home."

He did, and she put it out on the side porch until after supper.

After the dishes were done, Grandmother decided she had better have a look at the turkey in case it had pin-feathers, so she could get it ready for morning.

Grandfather was in the library and Bun was cranking the music box in the hall and I was seeing how I would look in Aunt Margaret's new red velvet hat, when the house shook from iron roof-railing to dirt root-cellar with blood-curdling screams. Grandfather got there first. Even he had heard.

Grandmother was standing like a statue pointing into the box at what seemed to be a skinned monkey with its tail wrapped around its neck.

Grandfather took one look and started to laugh. Grandmother went limp and began to cry.

He said, "You know, that's pretty nice of Doc. He's gone out hunting and got Sam a 'possum for Thanksgiving."

" 'Possum!" Grandmother's eyes were as round and blue as bachelor's-buttons. "Get that thing out of here!"

So Grandfather did. He took it over to Sam's, and apologized for the mistake.

Sam was touched that Doc Mullican had gone out and treed him a 'possum.

They both knew that Doc would rather hunt 'coon and 'possum than eat, but his gesture showed appreciation for all Sam did around Doc's office just the same.

Emil Schimmelpfennig's was still open, it being the night before Thanksgiving, but all the turkeys were gone. So Grandfather got the biggest goose Emil had. Grandmother was pleased with that. Uncle Willie was fond of goose because it was so colonial. It didn't agree with Aunt Belle and usually gave her an attack, but Grandmother had a slice of country ham she could give her. As for the goose grease, Grandmother would get enough out of the bird to rub on our chests the whole winter long. We saw to it that we needed greasing as little as possible, but it was always there in a crock on the side porch, just in case, and as a constant threat to the feckless.

We did have a Poor Farm—the bogeyman-land of all God-fearing people. It may not have been a retirement paradise, but it turned out to be not such a bad place after all.

It had never occurred to us that we might tangle with this refuge of the unwary, but we did once.

Auntie Marsh was a dear little old lady with a past. She lived with her son Davey in a little house provided for her in the mysterious way that things sometimes came to pass. Doc Mullican had a similar kind of real-estate tenure. The house he lived in with Cora B. and his five beautiful little girls really belonged to Simpson College, which rented the place to Doc for his brood and, when the rent fell irrecoverably behind, carried him along on the books for years. If Doc couldn't pay he couldn't pay. Certainly no one would have expected the college to turn Simon Legree and put the

Mullicans out in the road. Every year or so the
Treasurer would call on Doc and ask him to pay up,
and Doc would say he would as soon as he could, and
that satisfied all concerned.

That was a good deal the way it was with Auntie
Marsh's little house.

There were several stories about Auntie Marsh.
She was a lady born, that was for sure. She could bake
angel cakes a foot high, sew like a Paris designer,
nurse the sick, and baby-sit a whole family of young
ones when their mother got the chance to go to St.
Louis with their father. And still Auntie Marsh lived
off the land. Grandfather knew all about her, and did
mysterious legal business for her. There were several
schools of thought about Auntie Marsh. One was that
she had killed her husband (she was an unerring shot).
Another was that she had run away with her father's
stable-boy (she could gallop side-saddle). But the
most popular story was that she had married a scoundrel who had run off and left her, and that she had
come to hide away in Indianola when she was disowned
by her rich family. Another story was the same, except
that she hadn't married the scoundrel. Another was
that she was a bigamist, but that sounded too fantastic
altogether, so we never paid any attention to that
particular tale. Grandfather knew what the real story
was, but we knew better than to ask him.

Just the same, Auntie Marsh was always bringing
home-made bread over for "Brown." Grandmother
thought there was just nobody like her, and there

wasn't. Auntie Marsh lived by the Bible. There wasn't anything that could happen to you, good or bad, but what she had a quotation for it, and she was as facile with the "Old" as with the "New."

Auntie Marsh's boy—and we weren't at all sure he was her boy, really—was "not all there," and used to jump out from behind fences and make faces and say, "Kerslip, kerslap, kerslew, I'll cut your ears off, so I will. Kerslip, kerslap, kerslew!"

When Auntie Marsh died, her departure was attended by a kind of "mass effort" to do our best by her. Dr. Baker attended her in her last illness. Grandfather drew her will. She was dressed in black taffeta by courtesy of Charlie Meek, laid out in a casket donated by Mr. Orr, the undertaker, and buried in a pretty green corner of the Hamilton lot. And she was mourned by all, particularly those of us who had grown to gangling girlhood on her enchanting Old Virginia bedtime stories and her hot home-made bread. But something had to be done about Davey. Grandfather handled Auntie Marsh's estate, and when he said Davey had to go to the Poor Farm we left the table in a cascade of tears, flung ourselves on the grass under the willow tree, and reflected on the hideous hidden nature of loved ones.

Before winter came, Grandmother announced that Davey Marsh's birthday was coming up. How she knew this was one of the mysteries of her great golden-oak desk, but she had a way of coming forth with things like, "Thirty-nine years ago today Frank Stifler was made cashier of the bank at New Virginia."

And Grandfather would say, "At one forty-five."

On Davey's birthday we rented a jitney and rode out to see him.

To rent a jitney was in itself a world-shaking decision. Only direst need could justify renting a jitney, and one wouldn't be caught going to the railroad station in one unless he had something more than hand luggage to transport. On those rare occasions when we did get to go up to Des Moines to see Aunt Margaret's new baby or something equally momentous, like Aunt Madge's new husband, we were expected to lug our single suitcase by its handle uptown, around the square, out the college road, past Harlan's lumber yard, and finally onto the Rock Island platform—a good two miles any way you looked at it. Years later, after the train had ceased to run and before the rent-yourself-a-car service, we once were forced to hire a yellow cab to take us from Des Moines to Indianola. The feeling of profligacy was so heavy upon me that I slid almost to the floor and sat on my backbone, to hide my idiocy from the cows in the meadows as we passed.

But rent a jitney we did, and balancing a cake, among several other gay packages—two books from Grandfather, a pair of hand-knit black socks from Aunt Margaret, and a jar of a carrot marmalade from Mother—we took off for the Poor Farm.

Reading can sometimes be a dangerous stimulant to the imagination, and so it was on this day. I had an idea that we were going into a never-never land which was somehow a combination of Dickens' London slums and Stowe's "Life Among the Lowly." I expected to find unpainted tumble-down buildings, shrunken plots of earth bereft of grass, and crippled, toothless, cringing ancients hobbling about on sticks and dragging their rags behind them.

I am not at all sure that Grandmother was prepared for anything better. But what greeted us were broad green lawns with closely trimmed fruit trees here and there, a chicken-run full of fat Rhode Island Reds, a meadow with a sleek herd of Holsteins, and farm buildings painted red and neatly bordered in white. We saw a porch with rocking chairs, and men and women sitting talking to one another and laughing and carrying on and poking each other with canes.

The inside was dark and smelled of lye soap and boiled meat and gave me a headache. We went into the parlor to wait, and sat on a sofa that creaked, under a picture of Our Lord with His back turned to us talking to thousands of people while a little boy rummaged in a basket at His feet. You could tell it was Our Lord by the sparks flying out of His hair, and you could tell what was going to happen by the dead fish hanging out over the edge of the basket.

Pretty soon the matron came back, and with her was Edgar Allan Poe. He had on a black suit and a black hat and he wore a black, drooping mustache and one of Grandfather's black string ties. He didn't leer. He didn't say "Kerslip, kerslap, kerslew. I'll cut your ears off so I will." He sat down, and when the matron said, "Take your hat off, Davey," he looked at her like she was crazy and kept his hat on.

Grandmother talked to him about his mother, which I thought was indelicate. But he said that she liked it at the Farm and had been over to his room that morning to wish him a happy birthday, and he was pleased that she was so happy there with him.

The matron made signs behind his head and Grandmother nodded her head. For a minute she looked as though she would argue the point, but then she thought better of it and shoved the presents at him. He said he would take them back to his room to open them when his mother was there to see them.

The matron said Davey was such a help, chopping wood for the stove and all. I wondered if she knew about Kerslip, Kerslap, but decided to let well enough alone.

We all had tea then, served by a blond girl about my age who kept walking around Davey so she could brush her breasts against his shoulders. He turned and looked at her once and his eyes gleamed and he looked more Edgar-Allan-Poeish than ever. The tea was tepid and too strong and tasted vaguely of Gold Dust, which is a little on the order of yellow soap with just a dash of naphthalene.

Grandmother complimented the matron on the ginger cookies, which were very good indeed, crisp and thin and so hot with ginger that they burned your mouth. The girl giggled, passed the cookies, and leaned way over with her back to Davey so that he could have seen 'way up her to her Ferris waist. That is, he could have if he had been looking, but he was busy dumping one spoonful of sugar after another into his tea.

The matron moved the sugar bowl.

"Just like Brown," Grandmother said, and then I knew for sure she was nervous. "Always taking more sugar than he needs."

I thought that Grandfather would not have cared much to be compared to Davey Marsh, or to Edgar Allan Poe either, and after another round of cookies Grandmother stood up and explained that we had a jitney waiting, and out we went into the golden bright September sun.

On the way home Grandmother was silent, looking straight ahead down the dusty road, thinking about Auntie Marsh, maybe, and her secret.

I watched the fields of fat corn drying in their husks and thought, "Never again will I be afraid of the Poor Farm. But I'll never feel quite the same about Edgar Allan Poe."

And I haven't.

8

MY DEAR PROFESSOR

It is hard to believe at this late date, but none of us
Indianola girls (not even Dorothy Mullican, who
bragged so much) knew where babies came from until
our nuptial night.

Even those girls who had brothers were vague about the difference between girls and boys, and found it almost impossible to explain.

That there was a difference we knew in any number of ways. A physical difference was apparent in dogs, horses, cows, and cats, although it was hard to tell about cats.

But there was another difference. Grandmother used to say when she was "put out" with Grandfather that if she let the annoyance be special to Grandfather then it made her an inferior fool for picking him in the first place. But if she took the fault as universal to all men, then that put our sex a cut above the opposite one, and in our superiority we could afford to be charitable toward foibles obviously and exclusively male.

We had, now that I think of it, a kind of Noah's-ark conception of creation. Two plus two and so on. Male and female made He them. We knew the names and opposite numbers: cow-bull; hen-rooster; mare-stallion; sow-boar; jenny-jackass. But we were not at all sure of the variations or how they got and/or stayed that way, i.e.: gelding, heifer, steer, capon, filly, and the like. The polygamous aspect of the barnyard did not impress us one way or another, and the unique principle behind fattening left-over males for market was lost on us. The way we saw it was a man for every woman and vice versa, and when the proper time came they went two by two into their private arks, or bridal chambers. What went on there we wondered about at some length, finally giving it all up as being beyond our imagination. We would just have to wait to find out.

At a certain age it was not nice to show little boys your panties. At another, when asked, you married the boy of your choice. Then you could do anything you wanted to, like going up to Des Moines without an older person as chaperone, riding on trains at night as far as Chicago, wearing high heels, and staying in the room when older people were telling jokes.

Whatever had to do with sex ran, we were sure, as true to the rule as electricity did to the laws of physics. There was a cathode and an anode, and you couldn't get far without both of them, and both of them had to function at the same time with equal efficiency. And so it was with serious romance. Male and female plus the proper time and privacy.

When a man remained a bachelor we said he was devoted to his mother, which was frequently the case; or that he had been disappointed in love, which may or may not have been true; or that he had not found the girl of his dreams. One of these fellows was Professor Barrows. He was the devoted-to-mother type.

There was nothing sinister, scandalous, or suspicious about bachelors. They were just single men, that's all. If they didn't want to marry that was their business. Nobody analyzed, scrutinized, or cluck-clucked and tish-tished over them. We did not, as a general rule, feel sorry for them. Old maids, yes. Without exception they were objects of our pity and concern, but no matter what the circumstances we always felt a bachelor was a bachelor because he wanted to be, and that he could have and would have married if he had felt like it.

·If two men went traveling together it was assumed that they enjoyed each other's company and that they found it pleasant to travel together. A friend was a friend and a companion was a companion.

If two ladies remained unmarried and set up house-keeping together the situation was deplorable only because they were such nice people and it was too bad nobody had ever proposed to either of them. Sometimes one lady of the pair would be short, fat, pleasant, feminine, and a good cook, and the other would be tall as Athena, deep-voiced, strident, inclined toward tailored clothes, careless about the way she did her hair, and given to selecting those household duties that require more muscle than tact, such as spading the garden, putting up storm windows, shoveling snow, etc. This seemed to us a most happy and logical division of interests. Occasionally the two individuals developed certain eccentricities as they grew older. In this sense they were considered "queer," but in no other.

In retrospect, it seems that Grandfather's attitude, gained perhaps from reading the classics, must have been a little more advanced than ours. At any rate, it worried us more than a little that Grandfather was not more worried about Professor Barrows. One time, before Bun was born but when I was certainly old enough to know better, I ran in from the back yard to ask Grandmother something, or perhaps just to assure myself that she was there—even happy, well-adjusted children and pups need to make a security check now and then, just to make sure, every so often, that they are not alone.

So when I bounced into the house calling her name, she answered in a stilted, la-de-da tone, and not at all with her usual comfortably reassuring Iowa forth-rightness.

When I found her she was sitting in the parlor, smelling of perfume, wearing her new "fallard," and talking to Professor Barrows. This was a man I never did like. He talked through his nose and his eyes were too close together and he pretended to like me when I was absolutely certain he did not. For the rest of that day's visit I did not leave them, you may be sure, and although I knew I could not "tell" on Grand-mother, I did find a way to warn Grandfather that there was a fox in the chicken house. Providentially, on the floor by the black leather chair was a big wire hairpin. Sliding down off the chair, I surreptitiously recovered the hairpin. Then, by inching along on the waxed floor I got to the music cabinet, which was be-hind Grandmother and out of the Professor's line of vision. I knelt before the cabinet and, working care-fully so as not to arouse suspicion, carved, cut, and scraped a huge, bulbous "B" into the finish of the cabinet door.

Unfortunately for me, no one took it to mean Bar-rows, not even Grandfather. Instead of alertness and loyalty, the act was put down to wanton destruction. The "B" was, of course, held to stand for "Bo," which led to a tiresome repetition of that bit that goes, "Fools' names, like fools' faces, are often seen in public places."

The "B" lasted all the days of our lives, rawly emblazoned on the hard, shining face of the music cabinet, and for me, at least, it never lost its force as a warning against snitching.

Professor Barrows lived in a little one-story frame house out by the college. He was a pianist by trade and a musicologist by profession. He was "head" of the Conservatory. His standing in the community was impressive.

Grandmother had a real crush on him. You could tell this by the way she said "Professor," in a kind of hushed and rounded tone like a New Englander says "Beacon Hill" or an Italian says "Sorrento."

The Professor was underfoot more than we felt was strictly necessary. Since my warning "B" had come to naught, we children felt there was nothing more we could do but sit by and watch the slow collapse of our family fortress and way of life. But after a while— years, in fact—we got used to it.

We would come home from school on a bright, sunny spring afternoon to find the Professor sitting in a rocker in Grandmother's sitting room with a large folio volume of Italian painters stretched out on his knees. Grandmother would be sitting in her rocking chair, facing him, with a smaller volume of Raphael, or Cellini, or da Vinci on her knees. If they both rocked, they touched knees. They talked about art in the same sweet tone of adoration that Grandmother used when she said "Professor," and the pictures that came up in these art sessions were frequently full-breasted Madonnas with infants nursing, naked and exposed. Of course, a preponderance of the Italian art of this period depicted full-breasted Madonnas with infants nursing naked and exposed. But still, . . .

Then there was the music.

It is doubtful whether Grandmother had ever heard a symphony other than what was sawed out by traveling Chautauqua players. And her opera experience had been limited to Arthur Middleton and Father and the college glee club giving out with *Aida* and *The Barber* and so forth.

"Casey Jones," "The Erie Canal," and "He's Just a Cousin of Mine," which could easily have been provided by Mr. Orr's phonograph ensemble, were not precisely what the Professor had in mind. But Grandmother was sharp enough not to let him guess the limited range of her musical experience.

Sometimes the Professor would play the piano, and we'd know when we turned into the alley that it was Barrows and not Leta White. The Professor performed with the precision of a Conservatory graduate, selecting for his and Grandmother's pleasure bits of Brahms, Chopin, and Bach that were "way up there."

Leta, as has been noted, played with dash and daring. Often the same selections out of *Etude* would be played first by one and then by the other and then by the first one again, but we could tell the difference half a block away.

Leta made the marble bust of Beethoven on top of the piano jump and sway. The Professor always moved him back against the wall, where he would glare in white-eyed dignity. There was a certain similarity of features between the Professor and Beethoven. Grandmother must have seen this, and I am sure Grandfather noticed it. The Professor had thin, white hair worn on the longish side. He had aquiline features, and he carried his head high, so that he sometimes looked as though he had just smelled something bad, and at other times as though he had just given a penny to a child.

He was host to an exophthalmic goiter, which condition helped to accentuate his resemblance to the marble-eyed bust of the composer.

The Professor walked on the balls of his feet, which were small, and he affected brown, pointed shoes. His voice was placed in the treble clef, and he called Grandmother "Jenn*ette*." Her name was just plain Jennie, and we thought the Jennette was pretty silly and so did Grandfather.

Grandmother made the Professor tea, which she served in the best silver pot on the best silver tray, wheeled in on the mahogany-and-wicker tea wagon. There would be lemon, cream, sugar, cinnamon candy,

and fruit cookies filled with dates or hazel nuts or citron, according to the season.

Now that I know why Grandfather never bothered
himself about these matinee art seminars for two, I
also know why Grandmother had need of them. The
Professor, who was spoken of in absentia as the "dear
Professor," gave Grandmother a feeling of importance and sufficiency.

Grandfather treated her the way he wanted to treat
a wife, with love and loyalty, respect and pride. He
liked the way she looked and the way she walked and
her quick, sharp wit. He liked to tell that before he
met Jennie he was engaged to another girl in town
until he went by her house one day and saw her underwear flapping on the clothesline. That finished him. He
would not marry a girl with so little sense of the
niceties of life that she would wear, and publicly display, unbleached muslin drawers.

Jennie, need it be said, wore undertrappings of
nainsook or silk, heavily decorated with crocheted
borders, Belgian lace, and tatted insertions through
which was drawn blue, white, and pink baby ribbon to
be tied in rosettes at strategic points.

Her interest in the arts amused him in the way that
he was amused by our "Queen's Hotel" game, played
with little tin dishes. He liked to tell the story about
the day he came home to find hanging on the wall in
the hall a new reproduction of some nymphs in what
he called "gold nightshirts" playing ring-around-the-
rosey against a gilt foil background. He walked up

to the picture, peered at it, and said, "Jennie, what's that?"

She said, "The dance of Hebe!"

He peered closer, then said, "Where in the world could he-be?"

"All right, if you are so smart," she said, "what do you think it is?"

He said, "The dance of Juno."

And she said, "How in the world did *you*-know?"

He thought Jennie was the cutest thing in town. He didn't need her to be profoundly intellectual. He was scholar enough for both of them. It was her flippant wit that he had found irresistibly attractive in the first place. She was a perfect foil for his own keen Irish humor, and this was the bright side of his love.

She, with fewer resources of her own, had need of being taken seriously. A man of more solemn mien would treat her less like a precocious child, and more like a grown-up woman.

Such a man was Professor Barrows.

Moreover, Grandfather's tenderness was a rowdy thing, a slap on the seat, a loud and demanding bellow of "Where's Mommie?"

Although there is no way to prove it, my opinion is that his love-making was vehement, intense, and to the point. He was, consequently, outspoken in his impatience with "mushy-stuff." Tenderness, to him, was a womanly quality, and public exhibition of affection was simply "lolly-gagging."

The Professor's nature was different—how dif-

ferent I'm sure no one now living is prepared to say,
but it was different.

Maybe they were talked about. I hope so, but I am
afraid not. It would never have occurred to anyone on
West Ashland Avenue that Professor Barrows was
going out to call on Jennie Brown for anything more
than a look at her art books.

Mrs. Buxton, on the other hand, looked gay and
flirtatious. She was, I believe, about Grandmother's
age. She wore rows of stovepipe curls around her face,
like George Eliot, and she bobbed her head at men in a
merry way which we were led to believe George did not
do. Mrs. Buxton married in turn three, or maybe four,
widowers as they and she became available. Not one
of these gentlemen was what might be called a dud.
Mr. Buxton, for instance, was the president and principal owner of the bank.

Mrs. Buxton, as she was called at this stage of the
game, was Dorothy Hopper's grandmother, and she
and Mr. Buxton used to sit on the front porch of
their charming gingerbread house, behind big bunches
of mock orange and bridal wreath and lilacs and snow-
ball bushes, and rock and talk and giggle and have
more fun. The curls, according to Dorothy, were real.
There was a difference of opinion about that, but everyone knew for sure that she had two dentures and a
glass eye.

Her first husband, a Mr. Carpenter, had died, but
not before he had sired two daughters who subse-
quently married well. Aunt Eloise was one of these.

Eloise had been a friend of Mother's and between this association and Dorothy Hopper's blood relationship we took considerable pride in Aunt Eloise.

She had beautiful long, blond hair and a sensational soprano voice, and when the time came she went off to New York to study music and married a millionaire just like that. After three or four children had blessed this union (and apparently Aunt Eloise produced babies as easily as she hit High C) she divorced Number One and married his cousin, who was richer and so on. In due time she had a large assortment of children who lived with a governess in a house on the back of the lot, and she entertained her husband's uncle (who turned out to be a Methodist Bishop from Atlanta) at parties where she served champagne and smoked cigarettes in an ivory and ebony holder.

Aunt Eloise was a Lady Bountiful from 'way back. She sent Dorothy clothes and money and phonographs and records and singularly inappropriate fur neck-pieces and all sorts of other things. Her sister, who was Dorothy's mother, also came in for a share of the largess, but in her case it was a matter of necessity, for in the meantime, Edith's husband, Harry, had run off with a horse.

That Harry Hopper was extant we knew for certain, but he had fallen on unfortunate days financially, and these somehow involved farm lands and horse flesh.

Before the unhappy turn of events which sent him into exile, Harry, who was a born sport and spender, had tendered the College a gym known henceforth and to this day as the Hopper gymnasium. Grandmother said she knew for a fact that the gym had ruined Harry. Grandfather said she didn't know what she was talking about, that Harry had been bailed out of his philanthropic hole. Whatever the financial story was, dead or alive Harry Hopper remained fresh and palpitatingly quick to those of us who did twenty panting laps around the balcony track ring each day. We also had at the Hopper gym a plethora of "horses" on which we performed such equestrian antics as we felt would please our benefactor and patron.

We had no real information about Harry and the horses. We got the idea more from Mrs. Hopper's tone of voice than anything else. There was a fine bronze statue of a horse, more than a foot high, standing in the center of the Hoppers' living room mantel. We had seen bronze castings of Lincoln and Franklin and dead men like that, but we had never seen a reproduction of anything alive, sculptured from life. The fact that all this work had gone into a horse was in itself intriguing, so it was difficult to keep our eyes and our hands off the mantelpiece bronze. It was then that Edith Hopper would imply, with a shrugging indifference to our meddlesomeness, that if it hadn't been for *that* she would still have Harry.

In the meantime, thank the Lord for Aunt Eloise.

Then, of course, there was Belle Banner, who lived with the cats. This was something else again. She had got herself in *trouble* (how, where, or with whom was never explained) but she returned to Indianola as damaged goods to live out her life at the corner of the square, taking care of her father, cleaning up after cats, and appearing in the daytime only heavily veiled. Even on the hottest summer days, Belle would appear in Schimmelpfennig's butcher shop enshrouded to the shoulders in a veil as black as her transgression floating down from her black straw hat. She wore black cotton gloves, too, and black cotton stockings. When we asked Grandfather what she was mourning for he said, "Her lost virtue." And Grandmother said, "Belle is not an object of ridicule, but a creature to be pitied."

Our father, with maddening irreverence, said she was mourning for the man who got away, but Mother said gently that Belle was eccentric and liked to advertise her one golden moment of abandon with a perpetual and visual display of repentance. Just the same, if a boy got fresh at a picnic out in Pheiffer's woods and moved over too close when you were on the blanket, or tried to put his hand on your knee, you thought of Belle Banner and sat up straight in a hurry.

We felt the need of a knight errant in these days. The boys around the neighborhood were just boys. It was fun to be with boys then and it is fun to be with boys now, but somewhere there must be a special one, and none of the fellows in the junior class seemed like candidates. Skating? Of course. Or tennis, or Epworth League, or the Candy Kitchen, or even picnics in Pheiffer's woods. But knight errant material? Hardly!

There were some older brothers—Byron Hopper, who played the pipe organ and who looked like a Greek God descended from Olympus, or Harriet Henderson's tall, dark, and handsome brother—but they had no time for little sister's pals and preferred, foolishly it seemed to us, girls of their own age.

Then there was the older generation, and this was old indeed. Aunt Margaret had still not found Mr. Right, although Grandmother was helping her in her quest night and day. We had a progression of balding, pince-nezzed gentlemen, among whom Dr. Taylor with his Sunday bottle of wine and his Reo roadster was a breath of Broadway. Aunt Margaret perversely favored Mr. Kize. Undoubtedly he had another name, either fore or aft. Maybe he was Something-or-Other Kaiser, but everyone called him Kize. He wore celluloid collars and his pants were too short, but he sure pranced for Aunt Margaret. When he came to call she wore her prettiest chiffon or voile dress (one that the Missionaries would get in the barrel sooner or later) and fluffed out her pretty blond hair, and there would be twittering and cooing all over the place. We never got an Uncle Kize, though, because of two unfortunate and unforeseen happenings.

Aunt Margaret wore oxford bows, eyeglasses that folded out from a spring over the nose. Kize, as has been stated, was a pince-nezzer. Grandfather's library was off limits for anything but reading, and then only on invitation, but one Sunday when the Des Moines Hamiltons were visiting and the house was reeking of children and rocking with rollicking kin, Kize called. Grandmother told Margaret to take him into the library. Grandfather stormed around the halls asking what they were doing in there with the door closed, and Grandmother nervously shouted, "Reading!"

This naturally led to the question of what they were reading, and Grandmother finally got mad, slammed the front door, and went outside to sit in the swing with Aunt Belle.

There was considerable tension around the place for the rest of the afternoon. Grandfather and Uncle Willie went to sit in the back yard and talk about Commodore Barney. At that time Grandfather still thought he was descended from Barney, and he was making his supposed ancestor count against Uncle Willie's Alexander Hamilton.

Cousin Max was showing us how the new Maxwell worked, and Cousin Hal was trying to hear what his sister Nina and our mother were talking about on the front porch.

Finally Aunt Belle decided they had better start back for Des Moines before the dust got too thick from the Sunday drivers, and everyone gathered in the front hall to wrap up in dusters and adjust caps, veils, and gauntlets.

Aunt Belle had just told Grandmother for the tenth time what a good dinner it was, and Uncle Willie had told Grandfather for the first time that he wanted to hear more about Commodore Barney sometime, when there was a horrible crash and clatter in the library. Grandfather reached over and opened the door, and there were Aunt Margaret and Kize in a heap on the library floor, their red faces sheepish as they looked helplessly up at the open doorway.

It didn't take a Sherlock Holmes to know what had happened. Anybody with half a mind knows you can't make love in a Morris chair. Somewhere along the line there is sure to be a sigh like a gust of summer wind, a grinding of springs, and a shooting out, up, or down of hard black leather parts. A Morris chair knows its master, and is as skittsy as a colt with anyone else. Moreover, there is on a Morris chair no purchase whatsoever.

It wouldn't have been so bad if Grandfather hadn't let out a big, bellowing laugh. "Reading!" he had to yell. " 'Love's Labor Lost,' maybe!" and then he whacked Grandmother on the seat and said, "Reading, Jennie! They just came to the end of a chapter." Uncle Willie joined in and so did Aunt Belle, and soon everybody was giggling and laughing and wiping tears away and bending over and holding their sides, so we went around to the other hall door where we could see better.

Kize picked himself up, grabbed his hat, and recovered his dignity sufficiently to stagger out onto the porch and make his way down the steps with his head high and his straw skimmer at a rakish angle. We knew he couldn't see two feet without his glasses, and his glasses were now dangling playfully from his lapel. He hadn't even paused to pull himself together.

Margaret ran to her room weeping.

We might have survived all this if Kize hadn't gone to Detroit on business soon afterward, and Margaret hadn't taken it into her head to win him back with a lemon pie.

Aunt Margaret was not the most practical female in the world about a lot of things, cooking in particular. She could make some things superbly, like blanc mange and charlotte russe and boiled dressing and things like that. Kize was particularly fond of her lemon meringue pie, so while he was plying his trade in Detroit (and no doubt trying to forget the deaf ogre of Indianola and his mechanical man-trap), Margaret decided to favor him with a lemon meringue pie. It was probably the pièce de résistance of her entire career. She packed it neatly in a shirtwaist box, wrapped it in brown paper and red string, and sent it forth via parcel post. We never heard from Kize again—not to this very day.

We had another maiden in our midst, Aunt Dot. Aunt Dot was Grandmother's younger sister, and she looked like an old-maid schoolteacher, which she was. She was addicted to travel. One summer Aunt Dot would go to Germany, the next she'd go to Alaska. Then she'd have a go at Italy. But her favorite place of all was what she called "The Golden West." This Elysian land included, roughly, the states of Colorado,

Utah, Idaho, Wyoming, Montana, Oregon, and Washington. After a summer in Switzerland, Aunt Dot
would reward herself for that pedagogical exercise by
cutting loose for three weeks in Cheyenne. This did not
make sense then, any more than it would now. All you
would have to do to know for sure that Aunt Dot was a
strange one would be to visit Lake Como, Switzerland,
and Newcastle, Wyoming, in the same year. No
further explanation of Aunt Dot would be necessary.

Grandmother used to worry about her baby sister
traveling around among strange men the way she did,
but Grandfather said there wasn't a man alive who
was brave enough to make a pass at Aunt Dot.

Later, when the evidence stacked up against him, he
said it must have been Dot who made the passes.
Maybe it was. Once, going out West on the North-
western, she was trying to get out of her corset in the
lower berth. Now, Aunt Dot was only five feet tall and
as bony as a shad, but getting out of a front-laced
"garment" from a prone position was something even
Houdini never tried. Anyway, Aunt Dot was a-tumbling
and a-bumping with the abandon of a seasoned lower-
berther when the curtains began to shake and quiver.
No one ever told Aunt Dot what she could or could not
do, so she shook the curtains right back at the upper-
berth complainant. That stopped the foolishness for
a while, until Aunt Dot began to take her hair down,
pulling out the pins and, in so doing, cracking her
knuckles against the under side of the upper berth.
This time there was a sharp rap from above. Aunt Dot

rapped back with vigor. With that, a man's head appeared upside-down over the edge of her berth, and it said, "Okay, lady, I give up. Will you come up or shall I come down?"

Grandfather told this story on Aunt Dot for years, with embellishments, laughing until tears came to his eyes, until one day she just got tired of it and went out to Idaho and stayed. There she met and married a rancher with a lot of horses and cattle. She got herself into plaid shirts, boots, and overall pants, rode astraddle, ran the ranch, ran the local newspaper, and got herself appointed postmistress. (At the age of eighty-six she was to keep a boarding house for bus drivers because it was such a long, hard drive from Salt Lake to Pocatello.)

When we used to ask Grandfather how about that, he would say, "Why, that George Smith never had a chance!"

On the contrary, it seemed to us that George Smith had been a man of rare discernment. There are some women whose personality does not reach its full flower before fifty.

While we were interested in the romantic fortunes of Aunt Margaret, Aunt Dot, and the dear Professor, these aspects of love seemed a little pathetic and quite Victorian. We were in hot pursuit of the red-blooded, black-plumed, dragon-slaying knight errant, and we went to great lengths to find him.

Some girls fell in love with Charles Ray or Wally Reid or Rudolph Valentino or Ronald Colman or

Enrico Caruso or Carveth Wells or Ramon Novarro or Reinald Werrenrath. I had to go and fall in love with Gene Fowler.

Grandmother and Grandfather had been on a trip out West, and had stopped off in Denver to visit Grandfather's Aunt Lizzie Wheeler. Aunt Lizzie had a grandson named Gene Fowler, whom she had raised. The stories about this one and his antics made him desirable beyond reason. He was tall. He was thin. He was handsome in an Irish way. His wit was sparkling. He had all the free-swinging ways of the West, and he worked on a newspaper.

Ruth Wheeler came to visit us, and I stuck to her like hard luck to the poor because she was a real first cousin of my knight in shining armor. I carried my crush almost to fatal lengths. Ruth had decided that the comparative obscurity of Indianola would make it a good place in which to remove what she considered unsightly hair growing too far down on the back of her neck for the fashionable upswept hairdos. She bought herself a preparation designed for this purpose, which was to be melted in a pan on the stove.

After it had melted and cooled to a tolerable temperature, this gray wax was to be smoothed over the offending areas and allowed to "set." It was then to be removed with one brisk yank, like adhesive tape, whereupon the offending fuzz would be removed by the roots, never to return. Ruth had some success with her operation, losing only small, irregular patches of skin and leaving a number of little red wattle-like patches all over the back of her neck. But since Ruth could not see how she had been maimed, she was delighted with what she supposed was the efficacy of the treatment.

She said I might use the wax that was left in the pan. Having scarcely enough hair from my neck up to cover my head, I decided to use the remaining wax in such a way as to enable me to henceforth appear in bathing suits and sleeveless dresses plucked clean as a stewed hen. Fortunately, Grandmother's resources were unlimited, and by her tender use of a straight-edge razor and manicure scissors I was freed from what might well have turned out to be a lifetime coat of beeswax.

Gene Fowler was ten years older than I, but he was twelve years younger than Mother, and this gave her the grossly unfair advantage of being able to write to him and have him write back. Sometimes I would write to him and then tear up the letter and flush it down the toilet, which inevitably stopped it up and brought Jay Bergstresser on the double.

Sometimes I would get as far as the post office with my carefully worded formal "address," then lose my nerve, stuff the letter down the front of my middy blouse, and light out for home, feeling as certain then as I do now that Gene Fowler would only be mystified at hearing from this daughter of a great grandmother's great granddaughter—especially since he had never set eyes on me.

Mother recited Gene's poetry and people sent

Grandfather clippings of Gene's articles in the Denver papers, and our pride welled up at this wonder of wonders, a successful writer among our family connections. Then a sour note rang out. Gene began to write about his grandmother, Aunt Lizzie Wheeler, in a loving but clear-headed way that Mother thought enchanting and Grandfather found disrespectful. A battle raged around Aunt Lizzie Wheeler and Gene Fowler and Lizzie's husband, Norman. The more Grandfather stormed the more Mother quoted, and the harder I fell in love.

Eventually Gene married Agnes, went to work for Mr. Hearst and the movies, and wrote books that Mother memorized and made everyone else she knew read whether they wanted to or not.

When *Trumpet in the Dust* was published Grandfather disowned Gene for good, mostly over the part where Granner made old William live in the cellar, because everyone who knew them was convinced that this was really Aunt Lizzie and Uncle Norm put on paper. Grandmother said Grandfather's side was ever a traitorous lot.

Some time in the "between" days, though, Gene wrote to Mother:

> The life of ages lives in me,
> The way they went is where I trod;
> The One they worshipped is our God;
> Where fell the rose, its seedlings nod.

And she replied to him in part:

You asked me to quote you the little rhyme which Grandfather Parrott composed for my father. Papa says, "I have already told you that Grandfather Parrott and most of the family left their homes in Ohio for Kansas in April 1859. Well, a few days before they took the train for their western home, Father took a team and spring wagon and drove our family over to pay a parting and farewell visit to Grandfather's.

"We arrived at the old Parrott farm in due time, and I remember that there was quite a company there, but I do not remember their faces. After night, however, we all sat around a great fireplace in which one or two rather large logs were blazing up so that the room was thoroughly lighted. Grandfather had his coat off, and I noticed that he had a colored shirt, and I think the back of his waistcoat was of red flannel. His hair was a little long and was gray. He was a heavy man, and I think he would be called chunky. He took me on his knee, and petted and fondled me in a loving and affectionate manner, and after a while he began to compose the little couplet, making my name a part of it. This is what he composed, and he told me to repeat it over after him time and again until I could repeat it, young as I was, and he admonished me that I must never forget it,

Oswell Chase, by Heaven's Grace,
Will keep the faith and win the race.
It was no doubt suggested to him by the sentence of St. Paul."

The chunky man with the long gray hair and the red back to his waistcoat was your grandfather, too.

Sincerely,
Gertrude.

9

THE SECRET

One summer night, when the July flies were buzzing in the maple trees and the robins and blue jays were making their final fluttering peeps for the day, Grandfather and I were sitting on the side porch watching the

brilliant blue-pink sky to the west. We often did this on
summer nights, sitting quietly or chatting until the last
light faded and the stars shone clear in a field of
black velvet.

But I had something rather special in mind that
night. I studied his face for a moment and said clearly,
"Grandfather, will you tell me about Great-grandmother Hamilton?" Then I waited, wondering if he
thought me old enough to know the secret, or if he
still considered me a child.

He rocked awhile in the old black rocker, which was
the only thing he had that was hers, and finally said,
"What would you like to know?"

"What was she like?" I asked.

After a bit he said, "She had been in business about
four years when I came to Indianola to study law. She
never went out very much. It was Mary Hasty who
took me home with her one noon from the post office,
saying I looked like a good meal wouldn't hurt me
any. Minerva Hamilton was a little woman and a
happy woman. People from all over came to sit in the
back room of her hat shop and talk about their troubles.
She never seemed to offer advice so much as she just
listened. She was the most beloved woman I ever knew.
When she died there were so many people in the church
a lot of them had to stand outside on the grass and the
funeral cortege was so long the hearse got to the
cemetery before the last carriage had pulled away
from in front of the church. She was only forty-five
when she died, and not a gray hair in her head.

"But you have to know a little about David Hallam to get the straight of the story," he said. And this is what he told me:

Iowa was only eight years old as a state when David Hallam found it. Iowa needed men like David Hallam, and Hallam needed broad, new fertile fields for his own.

He was born in Washington County, Pennsylvania, on the twenty-third of August, 1810, the son and grandson of Revolutionary War soldiers.

By the time he was twenty-one years of age he owned fifteen hundred acres of Ohio land free and clear, had built himself a two-story, center-hall brick house with a curving two-tone walnut stairway, and he was building up a herd of livestock the likes of which had never been seen west of the Ohio river.

He was far too busy to bother about book learning, and besides there were plenty of other Hallams eager to be bookish and poor. He walked with a swagger and he spoke with authority, and there wasn't much he couldn't find an answer for.

David Hallam was a snob of the worst kind—patronizing, imperious, and condescending. A sense of humor might have saved him from himself, but lacking this there was nothing to keep David from becoming richer, more powerful, and more proudly important than anybody else. He took himself seriously, and so he forged on the same anvil the ladder to his success and the cage of his imprisonment.

The Hallams were not so much illustrious as determined. Jacobites, they held to their convictions. "Stubborn" their wives called them. "Uncompromising" they thought of themselves as being.

If they had lost with James at the Boyne, they had won with Washington in the West. And neither victory nor defeat had been tarnished by compromise.

David Hallam was also pleased to remember that his grandmother had been Isabelle Fell of Fell's Landing (later Baltimore), and that his mother was a Voorhees.

His young wife, Margaret, whom he adored, had distinguished family connections, too, back East. The Heslips of Chester County, the Flemings from the Eastern Shore, the Hopes who lived along the Brandywine, and the Vances of Virginia were her people.

It wasn't everybody, even in 1832, that could trace his American heritage back to the reign of William and Mary. Nor was it the usual thing for a young man in his early twenties to own land beyond the reach of his eyes, cattle more than he could number, servants, horses, sheep, and a wife so young and beautiful people stopped their carriages to stare after her. People had better not go looking for humility in such a man. Humility is a lesson learned, not a gift bestowed. David Hallam had all the gifts, but he had learned none of the lessons.

Margaret's first baby was a girl, and David was delighted. Being a stock farmer, he set a higher value on females than is common among professions not dependent on procreation. He named the baby Mi-

nerva Monina, and was happy to see that she favored
the Hallam side of the family. Her eyes were blue and
her hair was brown and her skin was as white and pink
as good English skin should be.

The next child was a boy, called Thomas after his
grandfather, the Revolutionary soldier.

The third was a girl born dead, and she took her
mother with her.

David Hallam could not believe it.

He could not believe that this could happen to him.
There had been some tragic mistake somewhere. Surely
the Lord would not so forsake him.

David's widowed mother came to raise the children.
Minerva was six and Thomas was three.

God had compensated Sally Hallam for her plain
looks by giving her a voice as warm and comforting as
a spring rain and hands as gentle as they were strong.
She had needed them. The wonder was that she wasn't
completely worn out by the time David asked her to
come live with him and raise his children. But she
wasn't. She had loved old Tom, and it had been better
than being an old maid.

She was Tom Hallam's second wife. He had eight
children when she married him, some of them older
than she was. Talk about God's will! Where could you
see it more than in the way she met Mr. Hallam. It
was at her sister Annie's wedding. Annie was marrying
a rich man's son, one John Hallam from out West
in Pennsylvania. Everyone else was dancing and
carrying on and she was helping to pass the cider and

the nut cake when she noticed an older man sitting by himself on the bench.

She knew that he was watching her, and since no one had ever watched her before she felt the blood rushing to her head until she felt dizzy, and when she went to the spring house for more cider she let the laces out a little in her bodice.

After Annie and John had left there was great excitement and giggling about the shivaree. Some of the men took milk pans and some had brought harness bells from home. They could hardly wait for the proper time to descend on the newlyweds with horns and bells and clatter.

"You aren't going to the shivaree?" the man on the bench asked her as she went by to pick up the mugs. She shook her head. "Either am I," he said. But as it happened they both did go after all. Annie and John had a surprise for their friends. When the house went dark and the clatter began, John opened the door and there he stood with Annie, fully dressed, and they lit candles and had all the guests in for punch and pound cake. Mr. Hallam and Sally walked down to the cottage after a bit and toasted the young people sedately and then walked back to the big house, and though he did not kiss her until many weeks after, and then only once on the forehead, Sally Voorhees knew she was going to marry Mr. Hallam one day—she had known it ever since the night of the shivaree.

David was her sixth child, and she did not approve of him at all. There was too much Hallam in him, and yet none of his father's sweetness. It disturbed her not to approve of David. He was so handsome, so charming, so generous, so successful in everything he did. It was somehow disloyal to old Tom, who would have been so proud of his son, for her not to be proud of him, too, and so she was glad to have the opportunity at last to make amends. So she moved in with David and taught his children to read and write and do wonderful things with numbers.

The little boy was quiet, sweet-voiced and gentle like her own mother's people, but the girl was a meddlesome one, forever asking questions and fidgeting. But old Sally loved her dearly just the same, and was anxious about her on the days when David came and took his daughter away with him in the carriage or to ride all morning on horseback along the ridge.

After Grandmother Sally died and David had to get a housekeeper for his children, Minerva elected to spend her days with her father, and he, flattered by her attention, let her do it. It was a familiar sight in town to see the handsome young widower and his lithe little daughter come racing each other in to town on stock auction day.

Minerva was fourteen when the women in the family took a notion that she was too wild for words and needed to be tamed in a proper school for females. David knew when he was outnumbered, and allowed himself to be talked into sending Minerva to Hillsboro Female Seminary, of which Professor Mathews was the head.

The erratic education of the self-taught is a danger-ous weapon against formalized approaches to learning. Minerva, for example, knew a great deal more than Professor Mathews about anatomy, biology, zoology, botany, and Alfred, Lord Tennyson. What he had to offer in these subjects bored her silly. But unhappily she was just as bored with Latin, algebra, spelling, and geography. Her contention was that had she been the least bit curious about these matters she would have studied them long since, and since she was *not* interested why waste time on them? If it had not been for Goodrich's *United States History,* poor Professor Mathews might have given up altogether. They both liked Goodrich.

David occupied himself the first year Minerva was away at Hillsboro by making forays into Iowa and coming up with a farm here and a farm there. He could hardly keep his hands off Iowa. There she lay so green, so fertile, so expectant.

The second year Minerva put in with Professor Mathews was even less cheerful than the one before. First she got the fevers, then the chills, and finally her father came to get her, convinced to his own satisfaction that she had typhoid fever. So never after that was she well enough to go off to school again. Minerva didn't mind at all. She was perfectly content to stay at home in Sabrina, ordering the servants about, presiding at table, riding horses, trying on new dresses, running the farm, and having, although she did not know it yet, the very best time of her life.

Meantime David Hallam was so happy to have his daughter at home, so happy to see her happy, so delighted with his own ability to nip out to Iowa every so often and pick up a quarter section here and a quarter section there, that it never crossed his mind that Minerva might be having company when he was away.

Nor did it occur to Minerva that she should not see her friends and entertain them at home in her father's absence. She was certainly not his prisoner. When he was at home she spent most of her time with him because she preferred to, not because he demanded it of her. When he was away she had more time for her friends. This was not a complicated emotional problem at all, just a simple fact of a very happy life. When one is sixteen and pretty and the beloved child of a very rich man, life does not seem at all complicated.

A poor man, an unlucky man, an unsuccessful man, or one acquainted with sorrow and discouragement is not easily surprised. He takes as his motto, "Even this shall pass away," girds himself for the next stroke of fate, and is grateful for the sun's warmth and the loved one's smile.

But a man like David Hallam is a sitting duck for the arrows of stinging surprise, as he found out two nights before Christmas in 1849.

He had been tempted to stay on in Des Moines for a land auction coming up right after the turn of the year. There was some land that could not be sold under three years from territory date, and the three years of Iowa's statehood would be celebrated three days after

Christmas. Instead, however, he elected to come home for Christmas to celebrate with Minerva and the cousins. He was pleased, as he rode up the lane, to find the house decorated at the windows, with candles and lights peeping out from the upstairs rooms.

He jumped down from his horse at the back stoop and gave her a whack on the rump to send her along to the barn. Then he hurried up the back stairs and into the kitchen.

The cook, Old Jen, was bending over a kettle on the stove. She had a long wooden spoon in her hand. Usually when he came home Old Jen left what she was doing, made a deep curtsey, and murmured unintelligibly, grinning the while. Today she only ducked her face further into the steam from the pot and stirred harder.

A man knows when things are not right in his house. Nobody has to tell him.

He put his hat on the peg in the back hall and hung up his cloak. His dog, Major, sidled up to him and licked his hand with affection but no special show of excitement. Far off in the front of the house he heard the laughter of young voices and the delicate wheeze of the harmonium.

The house smelled richly of spice and roasting meat and the ground pine that was laced in and out the spindles of the front staircase.

Minerva heard his footsteps on the polished floor and came running from the parlor to welcome him. It seemed to him that his heart stopped beating when he saw her. She had never been more radiantly beautiful, and he closed his eyes as she threw her arms around his neck. He held her tight in his arms, thinking what a little girl she was. Her soft brown curls brushed his cheek and he could not speak.

Then in an instant she pulled away from him and looked up into his eyes, laughing. "I've a secret for you Papa! A wonderful Christmas secret!" she said, and she put her hand on his arm and tugged at him until he followed her into the parlor.

There stood a pale, thin young man whose face was vaguely reminiscent of something. While he mentally struggled to place the boy at the tavern in Des Moines or the ferry at St. Louis, Minerva, his child, was saying, "This is John Carmen Ellis, Papa." And then he remembered—the young man was the merchant's apprentice at the dry goods store. He had come, no doubt, to bring Minerva a new hat for Christmas. Minerva liked having plenty of bonnets. It was one of her extravagances. There must be a new bonnet for every occasion. This strangely greenish-gray young man must have just delivered her new Christmas bonnet. That was the surprise.

But the boy's face began to swim in a mist of Roman striped ribbon and pink and green veiling as Minerva's voice went on, quite distinctly, "John is my husband, Papa. We were married Tuesday. That's the surprise. You've a new son-in-law for Christmas."

David Hallam was proud of himself for many things, but one trait in which he took especial comfort

was not losing his temper in a crisis. "Never dignify
your enemy with your anger," he was fond of saying.
Or, "Anger controlled is a means; uncontrolled,
an end." He was full of bits of wisdom which he was
willing to pass along at the most unpropitious
moments.

He could and often did create scenes of titanic
splendor, but only when his point was to be gained in
no other way.

To Minerva's intense relief, and no doubt to the
young man's absolute astonishment, David Hallam
walked over to him, shook his damp, soft, limp hand
vigorously, and whacked him on the back so hard his
teeth chattered.

Christmas was as jolly as Christmas ought to be.

All the Pennsylvania kith and kin that could manage
the rut-frozen roads came for the holidays and settled
in for the winter. Folks from Illinois and Indiana came
to the parties and made a week of it. There was dancing in the parlor and games in the hall, and Old Jen was
so relieved to have been spared a bloody murder in
the family that she outdid herself in elaborate cakes,
tarts, cookies, roasts, fowls, cheese, sausage, and sideboard dishes.

The Twelfth Night party was the merriest yet, and
Mr. Hallam made the punch himself from a recipe
that had come over from England a century or so
before, where as everyone knew it had been the favorite of Somebody-or-other of great Importance.

It was at the Twelfth Night party that John Carmen Ellis, after his third glass of punch, decided to tell his father-in-law what he had in mind. In brief, this was to rent a small cottage suitable to his income as a young merchant clerk, and to set up housekeeping with his wife, Minerva, forthwith.

Mr. Hallam was most agreeable. He admired young Ellis' pluck and manly sense of responsibility, but: as men they must face the fact that Minerva was spoiled. Without a mother's love to guide her she had not learned the arts called domestic. She should have a home of her own, it was true, and one she should care for herself, but first it seemed proper for her to learn such skills as were requisite. Therefore, since Mr. Hallam had the big house with plenty of room and plenty of servants, why not stay on for a time while Minerva learned her lessons in cooking and scrubbing and housekeeping from Old Jen and the others?

After it was decided man to man that the best plan would be for Minerva and John to stay on in the big house until she might learn the domestic arts and he could save for the little clapboard cottage, David Hallam suggested that they not speak of this again. "Minerva," he told his son-in-law, "is sometimes difficult to handle if she thinks decisions are being made for her. Better not say anything about it for the present." Enough that the men understood each other.

When friends began to ask Minerva delicately when she and John planned to set up housekeeping, she answered firmly, "As soon as my husband is ready.

In the meantime, he's perfectly welcome in my father's house." But the months went by, and she sometimes looked ashamed when other women talked about their little domestic problems.

Little by little, then, the men's talk began to turn to the fortunes of the West—the far West. Companies were being organized and fitted out, and many ambitious young able-bodied men were riding West to seek their fortunes. It was as sure as Sunday that no ribbon clerk could ever look forward to supporting Minerva Hallam in the manner to which she was accustomed. The longer he lived in Hallam's house the more unlikely it seemed that he would ever consider taking Minerva away from all this to live in the pinching thrift of a clerk's estate. Minerva spent more for her hats in a season than he made in a year. He had known that, once.

Opportunely, a company came through Sabrina in which David Hallam had an interest. They were not going out to hunt for gold alone, but for lumber and range lands, silver or other metals. They were more investment scouts than gold-diggers. The captain of the outfit was by coincidence an old friend of David Hallam's from Washington County in Pennsylvania, and, providentially, the company needed a man to go along to keep the books and look after provisions.

The talk had gone on at night in the kitchen, where Minerva couldn't hear. When Ellis came to bed, the bright new light of day had touched the room. She had never seen him so happy. He told her he was a man at last, that he was going out West to make a fortune so that he could build her a beautiful house like her father's. She tried to tell him she only longed for a little home of her own, but his mind was made up.

And so Ellis started for the West.

There were letters for a while back and forth. She knew where he would be until he got past Lincoln. She did not tell him about the baby at first because she wanted to be sure, but by the time she was ready to write him, his letters had already ceased to come.

Then came word through her father's friend, the captain of the company, that John Carmen Ellis had died of fever in Nevada.

Minerva packed the few things she would need when the baby came and rode slowly out to Illinois to be with her Grandmother Sillick. There her baby came in September, and to everyone's great surprise Minerva had an easy time and the baby was as healthy as could be. She named the baby Sarah Margaret John Carmen Ellis.

It was a year or more before she dared move back to her father's house. Her grandmother thought it was because she blamed her father for Ellis' going on the western trip with the company. "Don't blame your father," she said. "He thought he was doing right."

"Why should I blame Papa?" Minerva said. "John knew what he wanted to do. He was doing it for us." And she held the baby tighter. It was the memories the old house had that haunted her. But finally she knew

she must go back, and so she did, only to find her
father in a lachrymose state of mourning. He was
unable to speak of the unfortunate expedition without
tears. He blamed himself, and his remorse was pitiful
to see. He bought his daughter little gifts of cameos
and garnet rings and proposed a trip to Saratoga or
a new four-gaited horse.

None of these suggestions had the desired effect on
Minerva. She was polite, solemn, and quiet, and she
chose to spend her time with her baby.

So Hallam wrote to Professor Mathews and asked
for the names of some of Minerva's schoolmates, and
surprised her with a house party of old friends. This
worked better than he had hoped. The house once
again rang with laughter and smelled of cologne. The
girls—all except one, that is—thought Minerva's baby
"too sweet for words," and took turns seeing whether
Aunt Lavinia or Aunt Willie would rock her to sleep.
Jane Roberts was a tall girl with the walk of a queen
and the square, determined jaw of a police matron.
She found all this excitement over a baby a trifle hys-
terical, and could not understand why more fuss was
not being made over Mr. Hallam, who was so fas-
cinatingly thought-provoking.

Jane stayed on after the other girls had gone, although Minerva told her father she couldn't see why
he had invited her in the first place. Jane had never
been any special friend of hers. In fact, she was far too
tense and determined for Minerva's tastes. But Jane

stayed on nevertheless, and during the long afternoons when Minerva was busy with the baby, her "friend" found it practical to ride with Mr. Hallam.

All of a sudden it began to dawn on David that his father, Thomas, had taken a new wife in his fifty-first year and had thereafter fathered seven children by her.

When Minerva discovered Jane's intentions and her own father's preening desire she announced that she would make it easy for them, and moved straight back to her grandmother's. But Jane Roberts was too smart for her. It was marriage she had in mind, not the warm creature comforts that danced through the midnight reveries of her graying swain.

David Hallam was good and lonesome now, and resentful that Minerva had gone away and left him and in so doing made it impossible for Jane to stay on —because, as she had said, her reputation was at stake. Minerva never thought of reputations.

Hallam had one good way in which he could show Minerva that she could not do this to him. He had reason to believe there was someone who appreciated his company.

On the night of the wedding there took place the biggest shivaree ever held in that part of the state. People came from miles around to serenade the bride with washtubs and washboards and milk pails. David made gallons of English punch, and Old Jen passed around trays full of hickory-nut cake.

One of the guests at the shivaree introduced him-

self as a stranger in town. Hamilton was the name,
James Hamilton from out Maryland way. His father
had been a first cousin to Alexander, and he had friends
along the National Pike well known to Hallam. The
two men were about the same age. Hamilton was a
widower, as Hallam had been until this gladsome
night.

Since Hamilton was not occupied with a position at
the moment, Hallam thought he had a proposition for
him. An exchange of cards arranged an appointment
for the following morning.

What Hallam proposed was this: Hamilton should
go on West to a small town in Illinois, one of many
places where Hallam had friends in important places.
Hamilton should put in his bid for the contract to build
the courthouse. Hallam would insure the bond and
finance the construction, taking local bonds as security.
There were three such towns wanting courthouses and
three such bankers owing Hallam favors. It looked
as though the new-found friends were in business. There
was just one other little chore Hallam asked of his
friend. Hallam's daughter, Minerva Ellis, was a young
widow living with her child in Long Point in the home
of her grandmother. Obviously, with his new family
ties, Hallam could not visit Minerva as often as he
wished. He would consider it a great favor if Hamilton would look in on Minerva now and then, just in
case she should want for anything. Hamilton assured
his patron that nothing would give him greater pleasure than to oblige.

When Hamilton came to call at her grandmother's, Minerva was polite but uninterested. He was carefully tailored and he smelled pleasantly of spice, leather, and tobacco. She treated him with the charming courtesy she always afforded her father's friends.

With Hamilton it was different. He had made a deal about which he was now much ashamed, though it had seemed an easy expediency at the time. He needed money desperately, having lost every penny in Chicago, and, being a widower, a promise of being attentive to a young widow had been neither in his way nor out of it. For a man of Hamilton's charm and background these gestures came naturally. But he was totally unprepared for the task as it burst upon his unsuspecting condescension that frosty Sunday afternoon. He had rarely if ever seen a more beautiful and desirable girl than this child of Hallam's. This fact alone was confounding. Then he was to discover that she had not the slightest desire or intention of marrying again, and that she considered him a pleasant old friend of her father's.

As time went along, however, it became clear enough to Minerva that Hamilton was paying her court and that his intentions were to be considered honorable. She found him much like her father in some ways, and since Jane Roberts had moved into the family home Minerva missed the long, comfortable hours of her father's company. It was true that Hamilton was twenty-one years older and given to fits of moodiness, temper, and despondency. It was at times like those, according to the aging suitor, that he needed her most.

Her grandmother pointed out that the baby, whom they all called Maggie, needed a father. Hamilton was tender, gentle, and attentive. She could not go home, and as dearly as she loved her grandmother and Uncle Samuel she did not want to live with them all her life.

So she married James Hamilton in November of 1855. Their first son, Willie, was born at Ancona, where Hamilton was building a courthouse. Then they moved back to Long Point, where Jennie—who was our grandmother—was born.

Hamilton had, by this time, got rid of the money Hallam had given him to start out with, and was in need of funds. Minerva and the children moved back in with her grandmother, and Hamilton went to hunt up his father-in-law.

Meantime, Hallam had begun to tire of the old family place in Ohio. He missed Minerva and the gay days when she had been running the property, but he understood why she could not come back—indeed, his wife Jane made it painfully clear. Jane hadn't turned out precisely as he had hoped, either. She was the type to grant bedroom favors and then exact tribute in a dozen little ways all day long. He was not sorry he had married her. She saw to it that he had bountiful reason to be thankful. It was just too bad things had to change, but change they had. Now there was no longer anything to hold him in Ohio, so he sold out and moved to Iowa. It was a good thing to do. A new state, a new family, a new house, fifteen hundred acres of farm land and fluid reserves. First he opened the banking firm of Hallam and Son. Then he built the Central Building to show his good faith. Naturally he was a founder of the college and a founder of the church. He was the richest man in the county. It was preposterous that he should be unhappy. But he was. He worried because Minerva was 'way back there in Illinois, missing all this adulation of a new community for its most important citizen.

It was no use to speak of these things to Jane. She was too busy with the babies. Nice children they were, too—Rose, May, Imogene, Artimsa, Grafton, and Claude, but they were little tads not suited to be the companion Minerva had been. Besides, he was getting on toward fifty years of age, a time when a man should be thinking of settling down with his grandchildren around his knees. The more he thought of it as he rode out toward that jewel of a farm called the Trueblood place, the more he fancied the idea of Minerva's living here, only a mile from town—a place where the little children could run through the falling petals of the wild plum trees.

So he sent Hamilton the money to bring his family West, and however Minerva felt about it there was very little else she could do. This was the move known ever after as "coming out in the wagon." There was Hamilton in his Chicago-tailored suit and his high hat and Minerva dainty and fragile and dressed appropriately in brown calico cut in the latest style. (I

wore this dress myself one time seventy-five years
later when I was a student at the College and the
town was celebrating some Old Settler's Day with a
pageant and tableaux and such. Pioneer and calico the
dress may have been, but it was none of your sloppy,
dowdy mother-hubbards. It had a certain dash and
chic about it, and it made me look a good six inches
taller, partly, I suppose, because I stood straighter.)

Minerva's grandmother packed up treasures like
the Hope family baby cap and the Fleming family silver
and the Sillick pewter, and she put them into a trunk
and tucked the trunk in the back of the wagon. She
was used to seeing people leave for the West. She
would miss Minerva and the children, but after all,
with all Hallam's land, it would be better for them
there.

Hallam had the Trueblood place all neat and trim
when they got there. The house had been painted and
there were braided rugs on the floors and wood all
chopped for the stove. Her father explained to
Minerva that he had not yet transferred the deed to
her because for the time being he needed all the land
he could get as security for his banking and loan
company, which would, he hoped, become the first
national bank in Indianola. Minerva understood all
this. It really didn't matter so long as she could live in
this pretty little house by the orchard and the merry
little brook and watch her children grow strong and
tall. She was twenty-seven years old. Maggie Ellis
was almost ten years old, tall, gangling and dark-

haired like her father. Willie was stocky and blond and full of plans, like the Hallams, and Jennie, the baby, was little and dainty and gay. It was a good little family and Minerva did not care at all that Hamilton was away from home so much in Council Bluffs or Spirit Lake or Mapleton or Red Oak building churches or schools or courthouses or whatever was needed.

The only thing that bothered her was the Indians. Her father thought it was so funny, Minerva's having guineas as protection against the Indians, that he got her a pair of pea fowls to strut and holler and carry on.

No one could be exactly sure of the day it happened, but it was some time around Christmas of '72, that much is certain. The way Grandmother remembers it there was a little snow on the ground but the sun was bright. She was old enough to remember, for she would have been thirteen years old that year.

Anyway, Willie and Maggie and Grandmother were skating on the pond. The baby, whose name was Myrtle Monina Dott Sophia Morrow Hamilton, was home playing on the floor while her mother worked down the pot cheese, draining the whey little by little from the fluffy white curds.

The skating hadn't been too good on the pond because of the willow shoots that had got caught in the ice overnight when the wind had been just high enough to make the ice choppy, and so they had all three seen the man as he came along the road.

He was tall, dark, and citified-looking, and looked

somehow out of place on the frozen road. He was
wearing clothes that were stylish enough but too thin
for winter, except for the muffler wrapped around his
neck. His breath made little puffs of steam in the air as
he walked, and he did not look toward the children.
Afterward, when they talked about it secretly, they
agreed that he had looked rich and preoccupied. They
watched him go directly up to the front door, which
proved he was a stranger, for everyone else used the
back door. He stayed a long time. Maggie said her
feet were cold and Willie said he was hungry as a hog,
but still they stayed on at the pond. Jennie took her
skates off and went to hunt witch hazel buds. She knew
when he came out of the house, though, because the
guineas and the pea fowls set up such a racket. So she
ran back to the pond. The man walked down the road
again, but this time he was not in a hurry, nor did he
look cold or out of place in his thin city shoes in the
light fall of snow. He came straight toward them and
when he got to the bridge over Cat Hollow Creek he
stopped and leaned against the railing as though he
had all day.

Willie began to show off, making figure eights and
skating backward. Once he hit a willow root and fell
over backward and hit his head on the ice, but the man
didn't notice what happened because he was watching
Sister Maggie so closely. She was a tall girl and had
been going some with boys, so she knew when a man
was watching her. She adjusted her scarf and then sat
down on a log and tied the laces of her shoes and then

got up and skated up toward the meadow with long, graceful glides that made her skirts blow out behind her like a dancer's petticoats.

After a while he put his hands into the pockets of his coat and walked back down the road toward town. They never saw him again.

But nothing was ever the same after that day.

Minerva rode in to town a day or so later and rented a store on the west side of the square, one with a house and spare living quarters behind it. Then, without saying anything to her father about it, she moved her family to town. No one but themselves ever knew exactly what transpired between Minerva and Hamilton when he got home from Spirit Lake, but it was soon plain to everyone that they were no longer living together as man and wife. She made a home for him, though, and continued to look after him. To Grandfather, at the time, he seemed a little glad that he would no longer be beholden to her father, and quite satisfied with the comfortable little lean-to room at the back of the lot behind the millinery shop which she fixed up just for him.

They moved off the farm in February, and David Hallam was in for the second surprise of his life. No one who knew anything at all about the secret had dared mention it to him, so he had to learn it from one of his clerks at the bank.

"Good morning, Mr. Hallam," the clerk said. "I see your daughter has gone into the millinery business, sir. Takes after her father, doesn't she, striking out for herself?"

David Hallam stopped still, then turned and looked at the young man as though he had never seen him before. The clerk was frightened by the look on his hero's face.

"Mr. Hallam," he said, "are you all right, sir?"

Without a word David Hallam turned and stomped toward the glass door labeled "President." He must have done some thinking in that office about the stupid yokel who had met him on the courthouse steps a week ago and said something about wanting to rent the Trueblood farm. And there had been Janie's chatter at supper the night before, about some people not knowing their place and doing things to embarrass their family connections.

At any rate, he emerged from his office some time later, hat on his head and swinging his cane, and went out the back way through the hall. When he arrived at the west side of the square he stood on the curbing and surveyed the front of the millinery shop long and intently, long enough for the courthouse crowd to see him, and long enough to let several talkative people pass by. The shop had two broad windows, and there were two handsome hats in each. He studied the hats for awhile. Then there was a flutter of white shirt-waists and brown serge skirts inside the shop. The door opened and old Mrs. Brisson peeped out. She took one look at him, tripped over her dust ruffle, and came within an inch of pitching head-foremost into the street. Hallam could have caught her, but he obviously had other interests. When there could no longer be any doubt that his arrival had been adequately announced he walked up the steps and into the shop, and there he stood.

A nice-looking, competent, full-busted woman in middle years stood in the center of the room, her mouth full of hatpins and her hands full of brown veiling.

"Sir!" she managed to mumble over the pins. Her tone was hostile.

"I don't believe I have had the pleasure," he said, taking off his hat with a flourish meant to be coldly sarcastic, but his temper showed in the redness of his neck.

The woman took the hatpins out of her mouth, pumped a little more air into her handsomely expanded bosom, and said, "I am Mary Hasty, the milliner here. You have just frightened away a customer. I hope you are prepared to make compensating purchases."

David Hallam's mouth dropped open. Then suddenly Mary Hasty said, "Well, then, hold these. That nice Mrs. Perry is looking at the hats. I want to wave to her." And she left him standing there with a long length of veiling over his own hat, a handful of hatpins, and a foolish look on his face.

Just then the curtains parted at the back of the

room and Minerva walked in, looking prettier than he had ever seen her, the ruffles of her shirtwaist making a soft frame for her chin.

"Well, Papa," she said, "how nice of you to help!" And she walked right past him toward the window.

That was when he made his mistake. He lost his temper.

He railed at her for leaving the farm without his permission.

He pointed out the indignities of being in trade, the exalted position of bankers, and the heritage of privilege which dated back to William and Mary. The madder he got and the more he pounded the floor with his cane the less attention Minerva paid to him. She whispered to Miss Hasty and she waved to people on the street and she did not listen to a word he said. Finally he shouted at her, "God dammit, girl. Pay attention!"

And she turned to him and said, "Now, Papa, stop making an ass of yourself."

From that moment on David Hallam lived on borrowed time. He never knew, nor did anyone else who ever heard the whole story, how he had kept from having a heart attack or a stroke right there and then. Never, in all his life, had anyone ever said such a thing to him. When he recovered his breath he took one look at her and started for the door. Every moment he stayed in that pink, scented room added to the ignominy of his defeat. But she moved to the door with the lithe grace of the accomplished horsewoman she was, and stood facing him with her back against it, holding the knob behind her.

"Papa," she said, and her voice was flat and sad and lifeless, "John Ellis was here. I wouldn't be your daughter, Papa, if I could keep on living on your land and taking your money after what you did. I don't hate you for it, Papa, but I can't forgive you. And you should be ashamed for what you did to Hamilton, making a bigamist out of him all these years. And the children, Papa. How did you feel, knowing all this time that you had three bastard grandchildren? Hamilton's not fit to work any more. He never was, really. You knew that. He should never have been anything but a gentleman. So that leaves me only what I know best— hats. I haven't got the education to be a school teacher. Sewing makes me nervous, but I like hats, and as long as the women of this town like the hats I make we'll get along."

She closed her eyes for a minute, and Mary Hasty said afterward that her face turned as white as the porcelain doorknob. Then, in a voice they could scarcely hear beyond the curtains, she said, "I guess you'd better go now, Papa."

"He never came back again," Grandfather said, "and when he died she closed the shop all day, but she did not go to his funeral.

"You see, old Hallam had torn up Ellis' letters, and had sent him a message to San Francisco saying that

Minerva had died in childbirth and taken her baby with her. He had made a deal with the captain to take Ellis away and intercept his wife's letters when he got far enough not to be able to turn back.

"Of course, Ellis was broken-hearted. He had no reason to come back East, then. When he finally did get back this way he naturally wanted to visit his wife's grave. But he soon found out there wasn't any grave, and he followed Hallam's trail to Warren County."

"But what did they do when they met again?" I asked.

"No one knows."

"What a terrible thing Hallam did to his daughter!" I said.

Grandfather leaned his head back against the rocker and was silent for a long time. A dog barked as far away as Flummer's, and a pump squeaked where Mr. Brewer was getting water, ice cold from the well, for his invalid mother.

"It isn't what happens to you in this world that matters, Bo, but what it does to you," he said at last. "God is the master of the house. He expects you to be vigilant in your housekeeping. And if you can manage to be gallant, too, so much the better."

He leaned forward and put his elbows on the railing, and looked at the stars for a long time.

"I'm glad that you're here with me tonight, Bo," he said at last.

"So am I," I answered.

Then he reached over and patted my arm. "When

you go upstairs to bed, turn to the Apostle Paul's letter to the Romans and read the eighth chapter. When you come to the twenty-eighth verse, commit it to memory. It was a favorite of your great-grandmother's. Like the stars, it lit her way through the night, and it will do the same for you."

I did.

It has.

(continued from front flap)

came around on the Chautauqua circuit, and if one of them turned out
to be a disciple of Robert Ingersoll
you could run him out of town. As
long as you weren't an atheist you
could say what you meant, believe
what you liked, and practice your
belief.

Dorothy Daniel grew up in Indianola in her grandfather's house
amid a legacy of cut glass, plated silver, patchwork quilts, stuffed birds,
everybody's baby clothes from 1738
on, and at least one bellylaugh a day.
Her grandfather was a deaf lawyer
with a lame dog and an interest in as-
tronomy. And her grandmother had
a secret that the children weren't told
about until they got old enough "to
understand such things."

Although Dorothy Daniel's family may remind you of your own at
first, their story is simply like no other
story in the world.

Line drawings and jacket design by Sam Kweskin

Wilfred Funk, Inc., 153 E. 24th St., N. Y. 10

CPSIA information can be obtained
at www.ICGtesting.com
Printed in the USA
LVHW081125090622
720770LV00004B/211

9 781013 307041